To my friend Jo

With Love and I ... *Ray Harman.*

THE LOVE
WE ALL SHARED

POEMS FOR THE PEOPLE

AN ANTHOLOGY

by

RAY HARMAN

HORSESHOE PUBLICATIONS . WARRINGTON . CHESHIRE

ISBN 1 899310.33.9

British Library Cataloguing in Publication Data
A catalogue record for this book is available from The British Library

First published 1999 by
HORSESHOE PUBLICATIONS
Box 37, Kingsley, Warrington,
Cheshire WA6 8DR

Printed and bound in Great Britain

PREFACE

Because of the success of my last book 'A Resounding Voice', I have been inundated by requests from readers to produce a further anthology. I little thought at the time of its publication that my kind of poetry would appeal to such a wide and diversified public; and I have been moved beyond measure that so many people found pleasure in sharing my innermost thoughts and feelings.

Looking back over the many years of my life, it is perhaps inevitable that much of my work will be considered by critics as being too nostalgic and sentimental. If that accusation is brought against me, I plead guilty as charged, for I believe that without sentiment the heart of this nation would pulse to a very muted beat. After all, nostalgia, besides being a praiseworthy abstract, is also a union of two separate Greek words meaning 'the return of pain' - and what a marvellous definition that is, for who is there amongst us hasn't felt again the bittersweet desolation of first love, or mourned the unfulfilled longings and aspirations of adolescence.

So if you are the kind of poetry buff who is unable to share the warmth of my feelings, you will find little to your liking within the pages of this book. There are no hidden meanings to discover, puzzles to unravel, or fathomless depths to plumb. Every poem rhymes, tells a story, and comes straight from the heart. They are about ordinary mortals who have overcome their difficulties and hardships, and have been lifted by my words onto pedestals of their own making.

There are only two poems in this book which have been previously published - 'Twenty Year Or More' because it faithfully reflects my time in the Fire Service, and was earlier printed in an abridged form, and 'Those Dear Sweet Days', because it remains my favourite poem and will be seen to have more coherence now that all its original verses are included.

Each and every poem in this book has been taken by me to the people of this country, and their verses declaimed from rostrum and pulpit. If they failed to evoke a favourable response, then they weren't deemed worthy to grace these pages. This book of mine is now open for your perusal and I truly hope that you will find as much enjoyment in the reading of these verses as I did in their composition.

Ray Harman

DEDICATION

I dedicate this further anthology of my poetic work to my brothers Dave and Idris Harman.

It was Dave who set the ball rolling by sending a number of my poems to The Anglo Welsh Reviewer where they were duly published under the title of 'Songs of the Valleys'. Many of these poems were later featured on television and opened doors for me which otherwise have remained closed.

When my first anthology 'A Resounding Voice' was published by Horseshoe Publications in 1995, it was Idris who promoted sales by appearing with me in 'Poems and Pints' concerts in my native Welsh valley.

I am eternally grateful for their efforts on my behalf and glad of this opportunity to afford them the recognition they so richly deserve.

Ray Harman

ENDORSEMENT

"Ray Harman's poetry is both moving and inspirational and the title of his new book 'The Love We All Shared' is a fitting description of the warmth and sincerity that flows through his verse.

I have no hesitation in endorsing his latest anthology and believe that this new collection can only add lustre to his already formidable reputation.

Max Boyce

INDEX

A PEOPLE'S POET

Friendly ladies of all ages
Sit before him in each chair.
Apprehensive of his presence
As he stands before them there.
They have heard that he writes poems,
They have come to hear him speak,
Hoping madly he won't bore them
As the speaker did last week.

People's poet, in his seventies,
Looks upon each upturned face.
Summons up his voice and courage
Sees them through a misty haze.
Starts upon his hour long programme,
Puts great power in his tone,
Tries to touch the hearts of listeners,
Hopes that these aren't made of stone.

All his poems tell a story,
All his verses sing in rhyme.
See him paint a living picture
Of an age back there in time.
As he speaks of loved ones perished,
As his spirits lift him high,
They all share his joy and sorrow,
They are moved to laugh or cry.

Lovely ladies, past their summer,
Travel with him to their spring.
Pick wild flowers on that journey,
Melodies of childhood sing.
See themselves with hair in ribbons,
Playing hopscotch in the street.
Sometimes skipping, sometimes dancing
Wings of pleasure on their feet.

Now the poet plays Pied Piper,
Lets his voice entice, ensnare.
Makes them follow in his footsteps,
To a land beyond compare.
Where the grass is always greener,
Where the breeze is soft and fresh.
Where the friends they knew in childhood,
Come to kiss, and then caress.

People's poet at the rostrum,
Sees the lovely ladies smile.
He is moved by their responses,
They will stay with him awhile.
Fame and fortune are for others,
He just wants to share his dreams,
Wrap his listeners in his verses,
As they flow in loving streams.

I am he who comes to charm you,
I'm the piper, I'm the bard.
I'm the shaper of your feelings,
I'm the sword that pierced your guard.
Lovely ladies of all ages
As you sit before me now,
Look upon this people's poet,
As he takes his final bow!

~~~~~~~~~~~~~~~~~

GRANDAD'S LOVELY BOY

When first our daughter started work, she left her son with us,
And we grandparents loved that boy, for it was ever thus,
It seemed a son was born again, for we were not alone,
As Daniel grew into our flesh to make our house a home.

My lovely wife had much to do, for work wont fly away,
Her many tasks absorbed the hours, as night succeeded day.
And though she gave him what she could, it still was left to me,
To weave the colours of his life through time's rich tapestry.

I watched my grandson bloom and grow, and thought the world of him,
Shared magic moments, golden words, until the light grew dim.
I even potty trained that boy, and changed his nappies too,
And poured my love unstintingly as doting grandads do.

Each day was like a Christmas gift, as smilingly he gave
His loving heart and tender soul, to make of me his slave.
He'd look at me through wondrous eyes wherein was mirrored truth,
And I who was so worldly wide, was humbled by his youth.

We sat together in our lounge to watch the tots T.V.,
And as each puppet jerked and danced, he'd snuggle up to me.
I didn't have to speak my love, and he was quite content,
To put his little hand in mine and share the joy we felt.

When dinnertime at last came round, I strapped him in his chair,
And helped to spoon each mouthful in, to see he got his share.
He cleaned the gravy from his plate and started on his sweet,
Which vanished like the morning mist, for how that boy could eat!

Sometimes he's open up the fridge to look for chocolate bars,
Or ask to get his garage out so he could play with cars.
He tried so many games at once, he wore my patience out,
Yet I could not be cross with him, or at his antics shout.

Then all too soon he started school, though echoes of his voice,
Lingered through the daylight hours, to make my heart rejoice.
No longer does he press our bell, yet every morn at nine
I seem to hear those chimes ring through the passages of time.

I couldn't brush his lips with mine, my arms could not enfold,
The babe had changed into a boy, the silver into gold.
He still would put his hand in mine and walk close by my side,
But oh! the aching sense of loss, I tried so hard to hide.
I meet him now, as he leaves school, most weekday afternoons,
His tousled hair unbrushed, uncombed, his cheeks like pink balloons.
His shirt hangs long outside his trews, his tie is all askew,
His ankles fail to hold his socks which fall inside each shoe.

My wife and I now play with him just as we did before,
His chosen game, Monopoly, the board spread on the floor.
He changes rules to suit himself, buys every lot for sale,
Then will not pay his income tax or ever go to jail.

Yet through it all, this truth remains, he's still a part of me,
A living bond that will not break whilst yet his face I see.
He dwells forever in my heart, he floods my soul with joy,
A gift from God, who'll always be his grandad's lovely boy!

~~~~~~~~~~~~~~~~~~~~~~~~

THE CHURCH MY MOTHER LOVED

My mother loved her little church,
It was her heart's delight.
She went three times each Sabbath day,
And every week day night.
She was the sisterhood's top brass,
She led the Girl's Brigade,
And was the loveliest Christian mum
That our Lord ever made.

She organised the chapel treats,
And outings to the sea.
Picnic lunches on the hills
With cakes and cups of tea.
The Girl's Brigade she took to camp
To make their lives worthwhile,
And every cloud upon their sun
She polished with a smile.

The concerts in our chapel hall
Were all rehearsed by her.
She mixed the acts like flour and lard,
And then would gently stir.
The little children danced with joy,
The male voice choir, sang;
And as this blend of magic worked,
The hall with gladness rang.

Her voice was like an angel's harp,
A ceaseless, molten, flow;
And lullabies that soothed our fears
Were notes gold trumpets blow.
She planted seeds of hope in us
And watered them with love.
Then placed our trust in that great King
Who reigns in Heaven above.

The little church my mother loved,
Has now closed down for good.
But every brick and every stone
Was nourished by her blood.
She was this chapel's heart and soul,
She felt each joy and pain;
And sinners who fell far from grace,
Were raised by her again.

My lovely mum, no longer shares,
The world where once she trod.
The angel harp that was her voice,
She plays with joy to God.
She always loved her sisterhood,
And led the Girl's Brigade,
And really was the greatest mum
Our Saviour ever made!

~~~~~~~~~~~~~~~~~

BRUSHED WITH GOLD

(To a cherished daughter)

It was her room so very long ago,
And echoes of her childhood linger on.
She was a young girl here, her name's still on the door,
For nothing deeply shared is ever gone.
Through every day her presence can be felt,
Her room alive with whispers in the night,
While ghosts of bedtime kisses still come my heart to melt,
For she was always lovely in my sight.

It was her time, a season in the soul,
She made the darkest winter seem like spring.
When she awoke, the dawn was brushed with gold,
and in its hush I heard an angel sing.
She filled my life, I say this not in jest,
As countless fathers all proclaim the same.
For she was born, a fairytale princess,
And I still bless the magic day she came.

It was her world, and as I made it mine
I saw that all was different through her eyes.
The grass was greener then, the air like wine,
As we together chased life's butterflies.
The flowers that we picked, those bluebells that she loved,
The daisy chains that sparkled in the dew.
The earth became transformed with everything she touched
As all the old was changed into the new.

It was her choice, the music she adored,
And yet to me it seemed an age apart.
Sometimes I heard her sing and, as her spirit soared,
Responsive chords were struck within my heart.
Her voice was pure and innocent, like God himself at prayer,
Each note enhanced by joy, or drowned in tears,
And so moved was I by this as I listened in my chair,
I seem to hear it still across the years.

It was her charm that made me love her so.
She had no guile, and joy shone from her face.
She knew my tread on stairs, and as I passed her door
She swiftly came to share a warm embrace.
My spirit touched the stars whene'er I felt her near,
No other flame can burn as bright as this,
And as remembrance comes, I brush away a tear,
With memories of the lips I used to kiss.

It was her room, and nothing has been changed,
For never will her loving presence fade.
She's married now, her life is rearranged,
And lovely children grace the home she's made.
Yet though I hear her crying through the illnesses she had,
Or laughing at my jokes for pity's sake,
I know I'll still remember all the times she called me dad,
For the dawn is brushed with gold when I awake!

~~~~~~~~~~~~~~~~~~~~~~~~

WE FLEW THE CHRIST STAR

When Christmas was worship in chapel and church,
When carols uplifted and God ruled the earth.
When the blessings we shared, were all faith inspired,
We knew that Christ's love was all we desired.

When angels descended and Wisemen had come,
When God was the Father and Jesus His Son;
When Bethlehem's birth was more than it seemed,
Then in a dark stable the world was redeemed.

When churches were open and openings were doors,
When all said The Grace at the services close;
When ministers waited to see out their flock,
Our souls were the Lord's and our faith was a rock.

When choirs were singing and singing was sweet,
When God lit the candles and trees in each street;
When bibles were opened, not buried on shelves,
We recognised need and we gave of ourselves.

When giving was loving and living was flame,
When joy was the night that the Christmas star came;
When hearts were near bursting from all that we felt,
Then Heaven was the manger round which we all knelt.

When God was a river and Christ was the flood,
When bread was His body and wine was His blood;
When no-one forgot Him or why He was here,
Then all felt His glory and presence draw near.

When God laid the table and Christ was the Host,
When preaching was power and faith was the source;
When homes that we entered had Christmas inside,
Then light was admitted and darkness denied.

When people were caring and care was concern,
When love was the gift that was always returned;
When we were all pilgrims where Jesus once trod,
We flew the Christ star to the mansions of God!

~~~~~~~~~~~~~~~~~~~~~~~

A FREE SPIRIT

A cat has to be a free spirit,
You simply can't make it your own.
At the drop of a hat it will leave you,
If a greater affection is shown.
They were worshipped as gods in Egypt,
Revered like Queens in the East.
For they are all civilised creatures,
Whilst man, at his best, is a beast.

Cats never put ads in shop windows,
To find missing owners or such.
They simply stalk off to an upmarket home,
Where the folk are an easier touch.
If they're fed up with rabbit or tuna,
Or don't like the strength of your milk,
They'll seek out some Cordon Bleu cooking,
And cushions of purest silk.

To birds in a garden they're deadly,
So swift are these creatures to pounce.
You can't take a cat for a walk like a dog,
Or give it a ball to bounce.
Their kittens all practise hypnosis,
And when you have started to snore,
They tangle your knitting like crazy,
And tiddle all over your floor!

A cat has to be its own master,
It's simply not true it's a pet.
It's programmed to be the most selfish of beasts,
Out for all it can get.
And if I should be reincarnated,
As some people think that they can,
I'd like to return as a kitten,
It's better than being a man!

~~~~~~~~~~~~~~~~~~

THE HALLS OF HELL

My granddad was a miner, and worked deep underground;
And though he looked for light down there, no light was ever found.
In utter dark he worked his shift, in dark he groaned and toiled,
And though black coal dust stained his skin, his soul was never soiled.

He sometimes worked a three foot seam, which was so low and thick,
He had to lie down on his side, so he could swing his pick.
Filthy water soaked his clothes and mingled with his sweat,
Yet still he kept his spirits dry, when so much else was wet.

The colliery down which he worked, was like the halls of hell,
Where he crawled blindly to his stall, then crawled back out as well.
The heat would suck the life from him, to dehydrate his flesh,
And though the air he breathed was stale, his talk was always fresh.

There were no pithead baths back then, where men could wash and change,
He travelled back to where he lived in filthy collier trains.
A splintered washtub by the fire, hot water to its brim,
Lay ready to destroy his dirt, but not the love in him.

He didn't ask a lot from life, he had no special gift,
A quiet smoke, a pint of ale, and friends to share this with.
Welsh voices singing were his joy, they bore his heart aloft,
Where all his dreams were edged with gold, and none were ever lost.

My granddad was a miner, and worked deep down a pit,
Yet still he loved the job he had, and was quite proud of it.
He doesn't work a three foot seam, he's in a six foot hole,
And sings in heaven with the saints, for God has bought his soul!

~~~~~~~~~~~~~~~~~

FRIPPERIES AND FOLDEROLS

Have you looked inside a nursery,
That hub of every family,
To see reflected from its walls
The cuddly toys, the coloured balls,
The rocking horse with padded seat
And stirrup-cups for tiny feet.
The Hornby trains, the cuckoo clocks,
The countless Lego building blocks,
And all those lovely Dresden dolls
In fripperies and folderols.

And there are other joys displayed,
Enchanting books, superbly made.
Wool animals sewn into rugs
And childrens' names engraved on mugs.
A Wendy house with rooms inside
Where noisy infants run and hide.
And seven dwarfs surround Snow White
On Disney murals dazzling bright.
That seem to shine on Dresden dolls
In fripperies and folderols.

So many times within that room,
The nursery cow jumped o'er the moon,
While Pooh bear climbed eternal trees
To steal wild honey from the bees,
As Humpty Dumpty rocked and fell
And Peter Pan raced Tinkerbell,
To where the evil Captain Hook
Held Wendy captive, whilst she took
Into her arms the Dresden dolls
In fripperies and folderols.

Nostalgic thoughts so bittersweet,
Make hearts of parents miss a beat,
For children age and youth is lost
As summer sun gives way to frost.
The rocking horse no longer swings,
The Lego plane has lost its wings,
But worst of all, now we're alone,
We miss each child and sadly mourn
The things they loved, like Dresden dolls
In fripperies and folderols.

Yet our grandchildren now enjoy
A cherished book, a favourite toy,
For there within their nurseries
Are all the things that used to please,
Like Wendy houses, clockwork cars,
Gold papered walls ablaze with stars,
With cuddly toys, a rocking horse,
And in the cots, of course, of course!
The wondrous porcelain figurines
That only yesterday, it seems,
Were our beloved Dresden dolls
In fripperies and folderols!

~~~~~~~~~~~~~~~~

ETHEL

(My tribute to a wonderful mother-in-law)

Sweet mother of ours, now dying of age,
The book of her life on its very last page.
Born at a time when Victoria was queen,
Who knows all the wonders this lady has seen?

Stretched on a bed in a hospital ward,
A colourless drip her umbilical cord.
Dependant on nurses for all her needs,
Helpless and lost as her dignity bleeds.

Visitors hover around her in bed,
But she hardly hears a word that is said.
Forcing a smile from a well almost dry,
As the world in procession passes her by.

Perhaps she recalls what the world now forgets.
Or pictures the dawn as her sun slowly sets.
Or sees children playing around her at home.
Or long, empty days when she waited alone.

We have to go back to the last dying days
Of a dark nineteenth century's birthday of praise.
When in the back street of her dear London town,
Ethel was born, a bright gem in our crown.

Child in a world of cobble paved streets.
Buses horse drawn, with hard, wooden seats.
Naptha lit markets with bric a brac stalls,
And star studded nights in the old Music Halls.

Soldiers embarking at Tilbury docks,
Waving to sweethearts in ankle length frocks.
Off to a war that they thought would be brief,
As they set off for France and the trenches of grief.

Zeppelins caught in some searchlights bright glare.
Bombs hurtling down through the fog laden air.
The screaming of children, the grief and the pain,
Buildings on fire in a world gone insane.

Charabanc outings to Southend-on-Sea,
Laughter and song as the beer runs free.
The arms of a lover embracing warm flesh,
The sun's burning blushes, the night wind's caress.

Memories thronging as she nears her end,
The love of a husband, the warmth of a friend.
She holds out her hand to a presence unseen,
And smiles her sweet smile from the face of a queen.

Her life is a rainbow, springing from birth,
Painting our sky and then falling to earth.
Leaving its colours engraved on our hearts,
A spectrum of wonder such loving imparts.

With thoughts safely stored in a room beyond time,
This summit of peace is the last she will climb.
She knows we all love her, for truth never dies,
And stores in her soul what she sees in our eyes.

Dear lady, so helpless, on that final stage
Of life's great adventure, from birth to old age.
Drifting through dreams of what once might have been,
Who knows all the glory still waiting unseen.

~~~~~~~~~~~~~~~~~~

REQUIEM FOR ABERFAN

Peacefully they dream beneath the flowers,
Time has no meaning now for such as these.
No clock can measure out their hours,
Death's calendar sheds pages just like leaves.
Their mothers' voices, calling them from play
Are distant echoes in a cold, damp grave,
Yet they are still remembered every day,
And treasured are the kisses that they gave.

The sun come up each morning as before,
And lovely is the singing of the birds.
The children who are gone will speak no more,
As others flood the valley with their words.
Each evening lifts the curtains from the stars,
But fails to raise the burden from the soul,
For though time slowly heals the scars,
It never makes the tortured spirit whole.

As parents hide their grief in childless rooms,
Old photographs are time machines well used.
Outside the purple wimberry still blooms,
But here the fruits of yesterday stay bruised.
Though thirty years have fled since love was lost,
And maybe thirty more to yet endure.
They can't escape the ever mounting cost
For payment on such debt is always sure.

The smart new school can never be Pantglas,
One black October day has seen to that.
The coal dust casts its shadow through the grass
To darken where the lovely lost ones sat.
Nothing will be quite the same again,
Though life may end, the hands of time move on.
Each rainbow paints the colours of our pain
Each sunset is a day of grieving gone.

The pit at Merthyr Vale has closed for good,
Its murderous slag will tarnish no more dreams,
And deep beneath the ground on which it stood,
The blood of many souls runs through its seams.
Its winding wheel will bring no miners up,
Or screaming send hope crashing down its shaft.
And as we mourners drain life's bitter cup,
Tears tumbling fall where once men used to laugh.

And though I have returned to Aberfan,
To feel the love these little children gave,
I still can see no meaning to the plan,
That sent so many hurrying to their grave.
"Why us!" the parents cry in endless grief,
And there can be no answer we can give,
Unless it be the finding of belief,
Beyond these narrow valleys where we live.

Peaceful lie the dreamers in their shrouds,
They'll never know the cruelty of age.
They'll never see tomorrows' darkest clouds,
Or ever find that life can be a cage.
Their mothers' voices shouting last goodbyes
Still ring beyond the grave to heaven's door.
Where listening children surely hear their cries,
To answer with their loving as before!

GRANDSONS THREE

Matthew is the kind of boy who likes to get things right,
A born again perfectionist, because he is so bright.
He knows the way the world should be, but worries with this thought
That none of us behaves the way, he really thinks we ought.

It's not enough to know just how, a switch can turn on lamps.
He wants to know the source of power, the wattage and the amps.
He doesn't see the painted walls, but just the wires behind,
That hold the alternating force that lights his brilliant mind.

Jonathan has different skills, though he's a worrier too.
Believing in the things he sees, the facts he knows are true.
Not always confident or brash, but this is not a fault,
For those who charm through diffidence, are worthy of their salt.

But I believe in Jonathan, I read this in his face,
The puzzle pieces of his life, will one day fall in place.
And when they do, stand back aghast, and watch his rocket soar,
The galaxies are there to reach, and he will starwards go.

Christopher is something else, mature beyond his age.
A born to win competitor, a spirit naught can cage.
He sees his brothers forge ahead and tries to slow them down,
So he can pass the winning post the second time around.

Potentially the world is his, I see no barriers rise.
The combination of his gifts will take us by surprise.
Behind that sweet, angelic smile, there lies a steady nerve,
And we should keep an eye on him, for he could rule the earth!

Three brothers then, of differing styles, who never quite agree,
Sharing both their parents' blood, with some bequeathed by me.
Perhaps they're not quite ready yet, but if they do combine,
I know I will be proud of them, for they are heirs of mine!

~~~~~~~~~~~~~~~~~~~~~~

THE GLORY THAT NEVER ENDS

We came to Montreux in the heart of the year
When the sun was ablaze in the sky.
The dew on each rosebud was shaped like a tear
That was shed by an angel's eye.
The Avenue Des Alpes led up to the town,
The shops on each side shone like stars,
Their dazzling clean windows with pride looking down
On the passing of fabulous cars.

We stood at the foot of the station steps,
The joy that we felt was complete,
For we were immersed in the glorious depths
Of a welcome both warming and sweet.
We rode in our taxi to where we would stay,
The apartment of Mahin and Ron,
And knew deep inside in the noon of that day
That the grey of the winter had gone.

Our first cup of tea was more like a prayer
As it christened the long journey's dust.
We felt as we sipped, a lifting of care,
As our holiday plans were discussed.
Happiness shimmered, then bubbled and burst,
For we knew that the morrow would dawn,
And thought of the things that we could do first
In the glow of the Switzerland morn.

At the start of each day, the first views we saw
Were the verdant, green hills smiling down.
The sun would leap over the shoulder of Caux,
Then fall on the wakening town.
Its glittering rays would light all the flowers,
Then dance from the lake to the shore,
So we could believe that heaven was ours
And warmth was a god to adore.

Breakfast, though simple, was more than enough
To power our first early walk.
A stroll hand in hand through a garden of love,
Where touch was much sweeter than talk.
The avenue of trees on the long promenades
Formed arches of green fretworked leaves
That whispered and sang to the picture postcards,
As they spun on their stands in the breeze.

Steamers swept by like grand dames of Montreux,
On their way to a stately ball.
Schoolchildren spoke to their friends on the shore
And were met by an answering call.
Cormorants perched on grey craggy rocks,
Their beaks slashing arcs through the air,
As fussy ducks fluttered their feathery locks,
And swans bent their long necks in prayer.

Kaleidoscope views down impossible hills,
As our train seemed to loop the loop,
Chasing its tail with incredible skill
'Round track that resembled a hoop.
Seeing a tunnel approach to the front
Whilst watching the train's other end
Sidestep and stumble, stutter and shunt,
As it twisted itself round a bend.

We took the long cruise, the upper lake tour,
To places we'd never yet seen.
Sleepy small towns with a special allure
That all were so dazzlingly clean.
We crossed from Lausanne to Gallic Evian,
Past yachts flying by under sail,
Then burnished each moment with gold from the sun
So memory would never grow stale.

Our evenings were peace from an angry world,
And blest by the red setting sun,
From lakeside cafes, long banners unfurled,
As tables were laid one by one.
Lanterns exotically coloured and bright
Were lit as the shadows grew long,
To blend with the stars in the gathering night
As musicians erupted in song.

We came from Montreux, with our holiday gone,
Yet nothing can brush joy away.
We left for Geneva, whilst still the sun shone,
In the heart of a Switzerland day.
By the shore of the lake our train moved with ease,
As we drank the last hours like champagne.
Embraced by the mountains and kissed by the breeze,
We knew we'd return once again!

~~~~~~~~~~~~~~~~~

IT'S ONLY THE SINNER

When sight has vanished for ever, when music no longer is heard.
When thought is a concept forgotten, when the soul just fails to be stirred.
When body and limbs cannot function, when eating's a chore, not a joy,
Then you are no longer a maiden, and I am no longer a boy.

When love is a pleasure forbidden, when kissing now ends in disgust.
When touching just makes you embarrassed, when blood is a river of dust.
When all of life's treasures are stolen, and the thief is the ghost of old age,
Then you know the drama is over, so bow as you exit the stage.

When all of your interests are buried, when dreamers from dreams are divorced
When yesterday chases tomorrow, and all of your actions are forced.
When family and friends are but shadows, and you must be helped up the stairs,
Then it's time to be reading your Bible, and time to be saying your prayers.

When the gate into heaven is opened, by One who is older than time.
When He has looked up your credentials, to see if you're classed as divine.
When you are transformed to an angel, and try your first wings for size,
You will know as you enter the kingdom, it's only the sinner that dies!

~~~~~~~~~~~~~~~

FAITH, HOPE AND LOVE

Paul's First Letter to the Corinthians, Chapter 13

Though I speak with tongues of men
And pour angelic words on you
But have not love, I empty sound.
If I prophesy with power
To try and make all mysteries clear
But have not love, no joy is found.
Though mountains move, propelled by faith,
And wisdom grows within my brain
But love comes not, I nothing find
Or give possessions to the poor,
And throw my body on the flames,
Yet have not love, no gain is mine.

Love is patient, love is kind.
Knows no envy, never boasts.
Feeds not pride into the mind,
Kills not joy or burning hopes.
Never knowingly is rude,
Seeks not glory for itself.
Makes the angry comment smooth,
Keeps no list of wrongs to tell.
Love rejoices with the truth,
Always trusts and perseveres.
Never keeps itself aloof,
Makes all evil disappear.
Those who prophesy will pass,
Wagging tongues will all be stilled.
Knowledge held will fade like grass,
Perfect love will be fulfilled.
When I was a tender babe,
I talked and thought and reasoned so.
But when I grew to man's estate,
These childish views I held no more.
Now the looking glass is dark
Obscuring much that I would see.
Whilst knowledge I but held in part
Will soon bring truth alive in me.

And now faith, hope and love are left,
Three wondrous gifts from Heaven above.
But of them all, by far the best,
Is all embracing, perfect love!

~~~~~~~~~~~~~~~~~~~~~~

CERIDWEN

To paint a portrait of my Aunt in words that ring with truth,
I have to fill the brush of life with colours from my youth,
When she was young and times were hard, with children to be fed,
And as her blood ran rich and warm, I'll paint her body red.

When she was born, her parents shared a love that conquered all,
But then her father passed away when she was only small.
I've often heard my mother say, that she and Crid and May,
Knew not a childhood filled with joy and so I'll paint it grey.

She lost her husband tragically when Miriam was a babe,
But battled on despite her grief because her heart was brave.
Although the road ahead was long, she never once looked back,
And as no ray of hope appeared I'll paint that period black.

But then she met my Uncle Dan and she was once more wed,
Knew happiness and sadness too through years that swiftly sped.
Her family was all to her, she had no time to dream
And as those days were deep and full I'll paint the background cream.

She lived in Quarry Road at first, upon the riverbank,
And though the waters lapped her walls, her spirits never sank.
I used to play with Bill and Tom until the sun went down
And as the summer days were hot, I'll paint my cousins brown.

My Uncle Dan worked underground though poor in health and strength,
But still a fire burned in his soul that life could never quench.
He laughed and joked to make us smile, his words were always clean,
And as he made sweet laughter grow I'll paint his outline green.

Well Aunty Crid and Uncle Dan and all their children too,
For good or ill left Merthyr Town as families sometimes do.
They lived in Cefn Hengoed then, upon a fern clad hill,
And as they thrived I'll paint them strong as those who loved them will.

I used to visit them at times, such days return with love,
We roamed the mountain slopes with joy, and from the crests above
We looked down on the terraced streets where people looked so small,
And as the men wore navy blue, that's how I'll paint them all.

We wandered into Fleur-de-lys and Ystradmynach town
We walked at times to Gelligaer past children black and brown,
For in a little hamlet there the piccaninnies played
And as their colours intermixed I'll paint them every shade.

My Uncle had to leave the pit, for in his chest the dust
Had set like concrete in the lungs as silicosis must.
The family to Hounslow moved, right near the famous Heath
And as great trees grew all around I'll paint a branch in leaf.

Through all of this, my Aunty Crid, stood firm against the world,
Was strength to husband and to sons, and mother to her girls.
She cleaned the home, prepared the meals, worked at the kitchen sink
The work suffused her cheeks with warmth and so I'll paint them pink.

She lived in Isleworth by now and so when wartime came
The bombs fell all around her home and life was not a game.
She struggled on as others did, surviving day by day,
And as this was a purple time, I'll paint the years that way.

When peace returned and life was changed, her children all had grown
And left to marry those they loved and she was left alone.
For Uncle Dan, brave to the last, had lost his earthly fight,
And as his spirit conquered pain I'll paint its garment white.

She married Arthur later on, and he was good and true,
Rebuilding all her shattered life as men like Arthur do.
They grew together sharing all, and though she was no saint
The sun shone down upon a home that I'll in yellow paint.

She came to Christ because she knew her life was not complete,
The grace of God came down on her and made the hours sweet.
With water was her flesh baptised, with fire was her soul,
And her in silver will I paint, and our dear Saviour gold!

Though now her health was fading fast, and Tom and Miriam died,
She faced the world triumphantly for God walked at her side.
The valley of death's shadow lay just one small step ahead
And so it coloured all she did before this life she fled.

My Aunty Crid had many faults, and this we understood.
Her thoughts were shaped by life itself, and life's not always good.
Yet she was changed by scarlet streams that ran into the dust,
The greatest colour of them all, the blood He shed for us.

Grieve not for mother, wife or friend, for she is doubly blest,
Her father took her in His arms and laid her soul to rest.
Believe you this, that if you come to God through Jesus Christ
The picture I have painted here is your eternal life!

~~~~~~~~~~~~~~~~~~~~~~~

WASN'T IT LOVELY

Wasn't it lovely, when people were bubbly,
And laughed so much more than today?
When a joke and a smile made living worthwhile,
And we were so happy at play.
We all pulled together, through dark stormy weather,
And friends were companions for life.
When no-one was harried and most people married,
And joy was enthroned in the wife.

Isn't it funny that words sweet as honey,
Just don't sound the same anymore.
When they seem insincere, as if clouded by fear,
And folk have to lock every door.
It all seems so strange, when did it all change?
Are we that much different from when
We shared the same feeling, a process of healing,
Which made us much happier then.

It is now tougher to hunger and suffer,
Or have we lost some vital spark?
The will to go on, when a loved one has gone,
And the light is replaced by the dark.
Surely there's pleasure, that we can still treasure,
A warmth in the soul that is hope.
For brighter tomorrows will banish life's sorrows,
When we are more able to cope.

We are a great nation, in need of salvation,
For somewhere a great cause was lost.
When we stopped the caring, the helping, the sharing,
And worried what these things would cost.
O! bring back compassion, which went out of fashion,
A long time ago now it seems,
And make us all neighbours, not alien invaders,
So we can rebuild all our dreams!

~~~~~~~~~~~~~

SHE IS A GODDESS TO ME

When I take my wife out dancing, my heart just fills with pride.
She looks as lovely now to me, as when she was my bride.
She's as fine as Dresden china, a breathing, wondrous doll.
And when I hold her in my arms, I feel I'm ten foot tall.

She looks so cool and dainty as she sits amidst the crowd,
I want to kiss her warm, sweet lips and shout my joy aloud.
She always takes great pains to dress, so she won't let me down,
And makes a simple floral frock seem like a ballroom gown.

Each day we share, burns like a flame, though fifty years have fled.
My spirit soars, my senses thrill, and bells ring in my head.
Folks talk of luck, but can't explain, the fortune she has brought,
The treasure of her endless love, a gift that can't be bought.
To me, she'll always be eighteen, her age when we first met.
Her smile lights up the darkest day, her sun will never set.
For I am so bewitched by her, so hopelessly ensnared,
My heart still bursts with thankfulness, for all the hours we've shared.

And as she glides across the floor, within my warm embrace,
She makes the hall a living shrine, the dance a feast of grace.
She never lets me down at all, her steps dovetail with mine,
And music, only lovers hear, sings through my blood like wine.

When I take my wife to dances, no words of mine could say,
How proud I am to partner her, in every kind of way.
No matter the dress she's wearing, or where she might happen to be,
I'll worship my darling forever, for she is a Goddess to me!

~~~~~~~~~~~~~~~~~~

BACK THERE IN MERTHYR TOWN

My dad craved nothing for himself,
A giving man was he.
Five foot nine of hope and trust,
Yet taller than a tree.
Bigger men looked up to him,
For he would hand them down
The lessons that he learned from life,
Back there in Merthyr town.

My dad was cast from molten gold,
Though riches passed him by.
His aura was a dazzling truth
That lit the valley sky.
Wealthier men took gifts from him,
For he would pass around
The jewels of his priceless love
In poor old Merthyr town.

My dad, he stacked long rails of steel
That poured from Dowlais mill,
And in some place beyond this life,
Perhaps he stacks them still.
Tougher men took strength from him
Because he stood his ground,
And wouldn't bend before the wind
In stormy Merthyr town.
My dad, he sorrowed for the poor,
And felt each blow they took.
Wept for them within his soul,
And gave them what he could.
Weaker men learned this from him,
That when the chips are down,
You had to grit your teeth and fight
In jobless Merthyr town.

My dad, saw life in simple terms,
To him, no wrong was right.
Hate could never conquer love,
And black was never white.
Wiser men saw this in him,
And knowledge in him found,
That they would store inside their minds
In backward Merthyr town.

My dad cared nothing for himself,
A lovely man was he.
Five foot nine of ailing flesh,
Yet stronger than a tree.
All his peers looked up to him,
They saw he wore a crown;
And ruled the hearts of those he loved
Back there in Merthyr town!

~~~~~~~~~~~~~~~~~~~~~~

ODE TO A BRAVE, LOVELY DAUGHTER,
TWICE LOST BUT NEVER FORGOTTEN

JOAN

I'll never hear her speak to me again,
Yet I will still commune with her in prayer.
I never held her hand through all her pain,
Or took the growing burden of her care.
When she was born she made my life complete,
It breaks my heart that now we'll never meet.

She was her daddy's girl so long ago,
And I would proudly walk tall at her side.
Dreamed how sweet and lovely she would grow,
Planned to be her mentor and her guide.
I smoothed the cares of childhood from her brow,
And though love lasts I'll never see her now.

Her children and her sister gave her strength,
No woman went more loved from mother earth.
She would not have us grieve for her at length,
Or give the child of bitterness its birth.
I think she would have asked no more than this,
That she be still remembered in a kiss.

There are so many things that I regret,
The touch of hands whilst walking her to school.
Her many friends whom I had never met,
Her laughing voice when someone played the fool.
The catalogue of maybes still unfold
As seeking still, I find no hand to hold.

Yet she has kept her grip upon my heart,
And lights the darkest chamber in my soul.
Her flame of living burned right from the start,
And all it touched will never yet grow cold.
From childhood days her essence still I breathe,
Though flesh might die, she lives, so I believe.

So let her be remembered, not in pain,
But for the lovely person that she was.
A rainbow full of colour after rain,
A golden crown and not a weathered cross.
We owe her this, that we go bravely on
To make her proud in that place where she's gone.

To both her shattered children as they mourn,
To Lynda and her family who cared.
To all who knew the loveliness of Joan,
To everyone who in her suffering shared.
To those who lit her dark, my gratitude I give
And I will go on thanking them as long as I may live.

The circle has been closed, her passing was the means
To reunite both daughters to myself.
This was a sweet bequest, a fusion of the genes,
A balm to heal the agony I felt.
And when my story ends, then Lynda's gift will be
That through her constant love, my Joan returns to me!

JUST LIKE A PSALM

I saw a caterpillar crawl
From my back door to my front hall.
Then picked it up, and put it in,
A little silk lined toffee tin.

I put a lettuce leaf inside,
For without food it would have died.
And when I had accomplished this,
It soon became a chrysalis.

The creature slowly decomposed,
With nature's help, metamorphosed,
As there within its small tin box,
It changed its pants and changed its socks!

And soon a butterfly emerged,
Prepared to fly, just like a bird.
So dazzling beautiful to see,
It won the very heart of me.

I opened wide my kitchen door,
My task was done, it had to go.
So taking off from outstretched palm,
It soared to heaven, just like this psalm.

" The Lord's my shepherd, I'll not want,
He makes me down to lie,
In pastures green He helpeth me
To make a butterfly! "

~~~~~~~~~~~~~~~~~

A FANTASY WAS BORN

From the rooftop of a building, in the heart of London Town,
I could see its ant-like people, looking up and looking down.
Some were gazing up to heaven for the answer to their prayers,
While others with their eyes downcast looked burdened with life's care.

Then as I stood there wondering, a fantasy was born
Of how these people would react if Gabriel blew his horn.
And when that last great trump did sound, if all the souls below,
Would leave the prisons of their flesh and on the four winds blow.

Then through the mist that cloaked my dream, I saw an angel stand,
Upon the highest city tower, a trumpet in his hand.
With one bold move, he raised it up and blew with such accord
That all true souls who listened there, looked up and saw their Lord.

A searing flash of burnished flame shot from the faithful's eyes,
That rent the curtain of the clouds and opened up the skies.
Where gloriously the risen Christ with thorny crown in place,
Looked down upon a world redeemed, by his abounding grace.

And from each rooftop there arose a splintered wooden cross,
Ten thousand Calvaries to show, where once our Saviour was.
That all who watched would feel the pain that washed away their sin,
To throw the gates of Heaven wide and let God's people in.

Then suddenly the darkness fell, and Satan roamed the land,
To cast his dragnet, made in hell, to gather in the damned.
The streets ran red with molten fire, their tarmac surface split,
And that red stream, that bore the lost, flowed down the Devil's pit.

A fearful cry rose from the depths and brazen cymbals clashed,
As one by one, the city towers, into the abyss crashed.
Until the only one to stand, was that on which I dreamed,
Not damned enough to go to hell, not yet through grace redeemed.

I'll never know how long I stood wrapped in a cloak of grief,
I only know that someone judged, the scale of my belief.
Not hurriedly or with disdain, but by compassion swayed,
As in my love for Christ my Lord, I knelt and humbly prayed.

Then all at once the dream was gone, and though I'll always crave,
To know if I was judged as true, I knew my soul was safe
For from that day I've walked with Christ by His shed blood reborn,
Content to let the last trump sound, from Gabriel's golden horn

~~~~~~~~~~~~~~~~

LOVE'S IMMORTAL SEASON

A time of laughter, secret notes,
And stolen, shadowed, kisses.
Of tender trysts on mountain slopes,
Bright hopes and fervent wishes.
The touch of hands, the toss of curls,
That eyes might better feast on,
This prince of boys, this queen of girls,
In love's immortal season.

On Old Penyard, and Darren View,
Behind each wall and entry,
By Queen's Road School, and Chapel too,
While close friend stood as sentry,
They dreamed their dreams of joy to come,
And never thought to reason,
For their hearts beat like some huge drum,
Through love's immortal season.

A time of sorrow, censored notes,
From wartime's shadowed reaches.
Of khaki cloth and landing boats,
On some barbed wire beaches.
No touch of flesh, no shake of curls,
No tender youthful teasing,
For soldier boy and queen of girls,
In love's immortal season.

I write these lines in happiness,
To bring to all who read them,
A glimpse of paths through tenderness,
For all young lovers need them.
And I can feel the quickening joys,
Because of this good reason,
My father was that prince of boys,
My lovely mam his queenly choice,
And I will evermore rejoice,
For love's immortal season!

~~~~~~~~~~~~~~~~~~~~~~

GUIDE ALL OUR RUNAWAYS HOME

He never came home, that terrible day, a boy who was sixteen that month.
He had gone to school at his usual time, and stayed there till after his lunch.
And then through the gates of his playground, he walked out into the street,
To vanish perhaps for our lifetime, from a home he had made complete.

We had loved him so much as a baby, loved him so much as a boy,
The sound of his innocent laughter filled both of our hearts with joy.
The way he would run to be cuddled, the smile on his cheerful face
Were pictures God painted in heaven, on canvasses golden with grace.

He had always longed for adventure, and wanted the world to roam,
His thoughts were of mountains and oceans, but never the quiet of home,
And though he would love us forever, he just couldn't ever stay still
For he felt that the grass was greener on the other side of the hill.

Now we wonder where he is living, or if he's alive at all,
For we've never yet had a letter, or even a telephone call.
And our hearts are so sad and lonely, and our eyes so heavy with tears
That we never can think of tomorrow, or look without pain down the years.

Maybe he's alone in a city, in fear, and with never a friend,
Sleeping in damp cardboard boxes, or perhaps in a Borstal penned.
He may be abused as a rent boy, or high on a pinch of cocaine,
And stealing to pay for his habit, again and again and again.

All we ask is for him to contact us, that we might find out where he is,
And if he's in some kind of trouble, that he should acquaint us of this.
We are here by the telephone waiting, and we look for a letter each day,
It's all that we're living for really, since he who was ours ran away.

And to all the other sad parents whose plight is the same as our own,
We offer this prayer every evening, to the One who sits on Heaven's throne.
"Take care of our lovely lost children, in all the dark places they roam,
Light a star as you did that first Christmas, and guide all our runaways home."

~~~~~~~~~~~~~~~~~~~~~~~

THE RHONDDA WAS JOY

I'm an old man now in his sixties
And I hail from London town.
Yet back in the nineteen-forties
When the bombs came tumbling down
I was sent as a child to the Rhondda,
A valley dependant on coal.
Where I lived in a miner's cottage
And cherished in heart and soul.

I can still see Paddington Station
With its hordes of evacuees.
Snakelike columns of fretful kids
Fearful and ill at ease.
With battered and broken cases
Or bags that had never been new
Carried by boys in short trousers
Or girls in their Burberry blue.

The engine resembled a dragon
Belching out clouds of white steam.
Its scales were a line of old coaches
All painted in chocolate and cream.
With carriage doors hanging abjectly
Like wounds on its liveried hide
And seats with upholstered cushions
On ruptured steel springs inside.

Our mothers and fathers were waving
As we all scrambled onto that train.
Children were screaming and sobbing
As if the whole world was insane.
Officials were trying to count us,
But they had to give up in the end,
As the guard blew his final whistle
And we went out of sight round the bend.

Through Reading, Didcot and Swindon
Our train seemed to move in a daze.
Landscapes of cattle, horses and sheep
Unfolded to our weary gaze.
We chugged through the long Severn tunnel
So deep that the train seemed to fall
And emerged into blinding sunshine
To a siren's mournful call.

Strange sounding names in the stations
Told us that we were in Wales.
Clouds brushed the tops of the mountains
And mist hid the heart of the vales.

We thundered through Newport and Cardiff,
(By now we were mostly asleep)
Then puffed our slow way up the Rhondda
On grades incredibly steep.

We arrived at our various stations
With officials calling our names
Then taken to homes in the valley
By people who met all the trains.
Each dark terraced street seemed in mourning
Each doorway the mouth of a cave
And we thought this descent into Hades
Was one further step to the grave.

And then at Pantlfor Cottage
A couple stood waiting for me.
David John Morgan and Ceinwen his wife
With smiles that were lovely to see.
They each kissed my brow and embraced me
And spoke in such warm, loving tones
That the ice seemed to melt inside me
For I was no longer alone.

The Rhondda was joy to us children,
Who had travelled from London's east end.
They made us all feel that we were at home
For no-one was lost for a friend.
The people were poor but happy
The men worked long shifts underground,
Yet their smiles as they came forth to meet us
Were the sweetest that we ever found.

I still travel back to that valley
Though I go now by car and not train,
But David John Morgan and Ceinwen his wife
Are friends that I'll not meet again.
But I visit their grave on the hillside,
Where forever they sleep side by side.
And thank God for all people like them
Who cared for a dispossessed child.

And though I am old, I feel wanted,
The folk in the Rhondda did this.
It's great to be loved in the green of your years
When you know what loneliness is.
And those Great Western trains of my childhood
Still take me back there so it seems,
As I lie on the bed that is memory
And go back to Wales in my dreams!

~~~~~~~~~~~~~~~~

PARTS OF A PUZZLE

Christopher, Jonathan, Matthew are brothers and grandsons of mine.
Who all interlock in a jigsaw, producing a puzzle in rhyme.
Each piece is a part of a poem, each boy is a segment of verse.
Three fretworks that make up a picture, the oldest piece fitting in first.

Jonathan, Matthew and Christopher together are more than a match
For any three boys I could mention, the sum of their knowledge is vast.
Each child is an encyclopedia, each chapter dovetails with the rest,
And what they can do speaks in volumes, whenever they're put to the test.

Matthew, Jonathan, Christopher (they're in the right order at last!)
Have faith in a king who is Saviour, and all of the power He has.
Each one has his very own bible, all three read a passage each eve,
And their prayers are all listened to gladly, for Jesus can see they believe.

Matthew will go on expressing the hopes and the longings he feels.
With Jonathan right there behind him and Christopher hot on their heels.
Each boy is a line in this poem, each verse is a sonnet of praise,
A jigsaw completed with pleasure, as every piece slots into place.

And we, their grandparents will love them, long after their childhood has fled.
Three gems in the crown of our living, three children at prayer in a bed.
And though they're like encyclopedias, which all need upgrading with time,
The bible they read is unchanging, and the Word is forever sublime!

~~~~~~~~~~~~~~~~

MY TWO LEFT FEET

Though I was born with two left feet,
I thought when I retired,
That I would learn to sequence dance,
To this I had aspired;
And though ten years have passed since then,
And I've come on a treat,
When I get on that ballroom floor
I still have two left feet.

Sometimes they make a fool of me
These two left feet I've got,
When one of them will start a waltz
And the other - a gavotte.
They're not too bad with cha cha chas,
The rumbas or the blues,
But the foxtrots, jives and saunters
Are danced by different shoes!

Each message coming from the brain
Is ambushed at the knee,
And so my feet just never know
What my eyes clearly see.
My wife, who has to share my steps,
Sometimes goes quick, quick, slow,
Whilst I myself go slow, slow, quick
Like a hamstrung buffalo.

There are people living now
Who've grown quite old and tired,
Through watching my strange style of dance
Fall short of what's required.
The lines have deepened on their brows,
Their hair has turned quite grey,
And all because these feet of mine
Both go their separate ways.

The leaders, whom we follow round
The polished ballroom floor,
Both panic when they see us come,
And exit through the door.
They can't afford to be run down,
They've got a club to run,
They're not insured against left feet
When all is said and done.

There was a time some years ago
(It happened just by chance)
In some fine ballroom by the sea
Where we popped in to dance.
My braces snapped and jerked my arms,
My steps became deformed.
Yet people copied all my moves
And thus the Twist was born!

I went to see a doctor once
Who tried with all his might
To change that wrong left foot of mine
Into a proper right.
For twenty hours he poked and probed,
And used his scalpel free,
Yet still each message from my brain
Was ambushed at the knee.

There are many people now
Who follow Dot and I,
Believing that our style of dance
Is something they should try.
They're to be pitied and not blamed,
Such foolishness is catching,
For they'll end up with two left feet,
With neither ever matching.

~~~~~~~~~~~~~~~~~~~~~~

THE WINDMILLS OF THE BLIND

(For a teenage son)

He is my only son, the boy my darling bore,
And in his mirrored truth I see myself once more.
Tilting like Quixote at the windmills of the blind,
I wish five billion sons like mine made up the whole mankind.

He dreams the age old dream, that love will conquer all,
I hate to see him brought up short, by life's unyielding wall.
Dear God! what happens to ideals when we reach middle age,
Why is it left to tender youth, to write a brighter page?

He writes his protest verse, and it's original to him,
Pollution, mass destruction, with the future black and grim.
He sees no shade of grey, or trees of hope in bud,
But paints in words of crimson, like the colour of his blood.

He feels for the downtrodden human debris of this earth,
Impatiently assessing what men's promises are worth.
He bleeds for victims slaughtered in the name of many creeds,
And sees in anguished, helpless eyes, the suff'ring hatred breeds.

The rivers ooze with poison and the planet's flora wilts,
Mutations happen, genes change, and nature's balance tilts,
He sees the hand of darkness squeezing life from earth's sweet throat,
And men in distant, backward lands, denied the right to vote.

Our worries are his nightmares, our gains become his loss.
Yet there across his poems, falls the shadow of the cross.
He knows with utter certainty in his immortal soul,
That we are doomed, unless God's love will reign from Pole to Pole.

He is my only son, and tender is his heart
Trying to build a bright new world, where love will play its part.
Tilting like Quixote at the windmills of the blind,
I wish five billion sons like mine made up the whole mankind!

~~~~~~~~~~~~~~~~~~~~~~

AFTER ARMAGEDDON

I saw the world's last tree today,
Not crowned by leaves but gaunt and grey,
Whilst on each twisted, leprous, branch,
Where bird and squirrel used to dance,
A fungi grew so loathsome dressed,
It wore a cancer on its breast.

I heard the world's last song this morn,
Nor from a bird inspired by dawn,
Not from a child, for youth had fled
And like the earth was long since dead,
As through the ruined homes of Man
The howling wind its requiem sang.

I picked the world's last flower this noon,
A mutant hybrid, ripe with doom,
No viscous juice within its stem,
Or pollen dust on petalled hem,
For on the radioactive breeze
Death lay in wait for honey bees.

I saw the world's last fish this night,
Its scabrous scales no longer bright,
Its mildewed fins and rotting jaw
Just like its tail, were festered, raw,
While in each eye of nightmare hue,
A nameless worm of evil grew.

I saw the world's last fossilled bones
Atomic etched on wordless stones.
No epitaph for loved ones slain,
Except perhaps the mark of Cain,
Or maybe remnants of a cross
Where once the hill of Calvary was.

I see no life beyond this day,
No trees or plants, no child at play.
But if the earth has long since died,
What frightful creature now defiled
Can write these words unless it be
Part bird, part fish, part beast, part me?

~~~~~~~~~~~~~~~~~~~~~~~~

THE FIRST AND THE LAST (For Kathryn)

Little one, little one, when you were born
You painted my life with the gold of your dawn.
A glorious grand-daughter, the first and the last
Who brightened my winter when autumn had passed.

I still see you lie, a sweet bundle of charms,
Just after your birth, in my own daughter's arms;
And I wondered how you could ever exist,
When it seemed you might melt in the warmth of a kiss.

Close to me, dear to me, warm and petite,
Your skin smelled of talc and your lips were so sweet.
You splashed in your bath and your slave I would be,
As you crinkled your eyes and smiled up at me.

Remember that first winter snowman we built?
Dressed like a clown in an old patchwork quilt.
Two pennies for eyes and a carrot for nose,
Such memories return when the winter wind blows.

Baby face, baby face, dimpled and soft,
Your smiles were my sun as I held you aloft.
Your kiss was a blessing, your touch was my world,
For oh! how I loved you, my sweet little girl.

We walked to the park on warm summer days,
As I kept you in check with a tug at your reins.
I pushed you down slides and rocked you on swings,
Flying up high with your coat-tails for wings.

Golden girl, golden girl, may time treat you well.
What I want for you, the heart cannot tell.
Be sure I'll be there when the clouds hide your sun,
A shoulder to cry on when stormy days come.

You are my daughter in all but the name,
She was my princess and you are the same.
We are a blend of late autumn and spring,
No words can express all the wonder you bring.

Grand-daughter, grand-daughter, don't let me down,
I've placed you on pedestals all over town.
Sung all you praises to family and friends,
Pray God this continues till memory ends.

For I want you to grow into virtue and truth,
An essence distilled from the bloom of your youth.
And need to know this, as your journey I share,
That joy and not grief is the crown that you'll wear.

Kathryn, my Kathryn, Oh! what I would give
To be close beside you as long as you live,
To see you grow up with your soul undefiled,
To be at your wedding and nurse your first child.

You now paint your nails and make-up your face,
But I still remember when you walked in grace.
When you ran to my arms with excitable cries,
As I happily drowned in the pool of your eyes.

Lovely one, lovely one, how you have grown,
Since you were a baby the years have just flown.
Tiny and helpless I cradled you then,
Oh! how I wish I could do this again!

~~~~~~~~~~~~~~~~~~~~~~

CANNIBALS

Did you know that man is carnivorous?
And where there's no creature to munch,
They have taken to eating each other,
And us, if we pop in for lunch.

They don't think that this vile behaviour,
Departs any way from the norm.
They will cut off a joint in a jiffy,
and eat you alive if you're warm.

Cannibals find us delicious,
Especially with cranberry sauce.
Succulent, tender and spicy,
To them it's like eating a horse.

They take out the bones and the offal,
Then boil us in earthenware pots.
Though they are particular in some things,
They won't eat a human with spots.

For pudding they have kidney crumble,
Sweet flavoured with liver and tongue.
The heart they will marinate slowly
In clusters of elephant dung.

They never use doilies or napkins,
They don't sit to table like us.
But they'll sing the rudest of ditties,
As they polish us off without fuss.

In this there is one crumb of comfort,
To Oxfam our residue goes.
And many a savage in bow tie and spats
Is grateful for civilised clothes.

Our shoes, if they're made of fine leather,
Make wonderful claret or hock
If rendered with sulphuric acid
And sieved through a sweaty old sock.

For myself I prefer to be eaten
By people with manners and style.
Who buy all their spices from Harrods
And their sugar from Tate and Lyle.

At least, if they burp, they say pardon,
Or mutter the grace before meals;
And never, not ever eat burgers,
Or pie, mashed potatoes and eels.

So if you've a choice, put your foot down,
Don't go where the cman eaters dwell.
Or you could end up in an earthenware pot,
That's hotter by far than hell.

I hope my example you'll follow,
Have baked beans on toast for your tea.
Let cannibals drool over barbecued man,
They won't make a meal out of me!

~~~~~~~~~~~~~~~~~~~~~~~~

DEAR HARRY

Get well soon dear Harry, we miss your happy face,
Those jives performed with gusto, those foxtrots danced with grace.
We miss your tender gentleness, we miss your inner strength,
But most of all, dear friend of ours, we miss you for yourself.

Although we've known you many years, it's just a smile away,
For we have shared the soul of dance, the sun that lights our day.
Each sequence is a corner turned, with vistas edged with gold,
That stretch beyond the realms of time, and bring us joys untold.

We know you must be fretting, now that you're told to rest
And though you long to dance once more, your doctor does know best.
We want you fit and well again, just like you used to be,
So Damaris and you are seen still following Dot and me.

We have a great respect for you and like the things you are,
The way you think of others first, the flame that lights our star,
The seeking out of ladies who sit lonely on their chairs,
Until you take them in your arms and match your step with theirs.

Our world is cold without you, we need your flame to burn,
So we can warm ourselves on you, when you at last return.
You are the essence truth distils, the universal friend,
Who stands besides the folk he loves, right to the very end.

You made our club the joy it is, and thus transformed our lives,
And we still feel your guiding hand, when Thursday night arrives.
You put us on an even keel, you made us feel secure,
A solid gold foundation stone, on which our dance endures.

And with beloved Damaris, you make a perfect pair,
The love that lifts our spirits up, the thought within a prayer.
And we look forward to the day when you will come again,
To brighten corners that were dark, like sunshine after rain.

Our dancing world will miss you both, until your voice is heard,
These feelings are not mine alone, I simply write the words;
And try to show in my poor way, just why we miss you so,
The sense of loss, the empty chairs, your absence from the floor.

So get well soon dear Harry, for you're our kind of man,
A very special person, who does the best he can.
We miss your splendid qualities, we miss your commonsense,
But most of all dear friend of ours, we miss you for yourself!

Born out of admiration and written from the heart by your friend always, Ray.

~~~~~~~~~~~~~~~~~~~~~~

BREAD FROM THE BOX OF JOY

I took the sweet smile from a young girl's lips,
I took the hard strength of a boy,
I took of the wine that a wise man sips,
And I tool all these gifts with joy.
I've looked in the eyes of the woman I love,
Who has shared these rich gifts as my wife,
I have stood on that hill with God's heaven above,
I have found the true meaning of life.

I have listened to Welsh voices singing,
I have cut at the black seams of coal,
I have thrilled to the chapel bells ringing,
I've been moved to the depths of my soul.
I have walked through the land of emotion,
And have shared with my own people there,
The love that's as deep as the ocean,
The joy that's as sweet as a prayer.

I have looked through the eyes of my daughter,
At a world I remember so well,
Where the tears intermingled with laughter,
In a way that the heart cannot tell.
I have sired a son with a mission,
To follow where Jesus Christ trod,
Inspired by the message and vision,
Of the far reaching kingdom of God.

I have listened to Christ's greatest sermon
On Mount Olive, far, far away.
I have knelt by His cross and whispered amen,
When my heart has remembered to pray.
I was there with the wine and the glory,
At that very last supper he gave,
I am here to the end of His story,
The soul our Lord Jesus did save.

I took the sweet smile from a young girl's lips,
I took the hard strength of a boy,
I took of the wine a communicant sips,
With bread from the body of joy.
I rolled back the stone from the Easter tomb,
And Jesus came into my life,
Where he walks through my home into every room,
To be shared with my children and wife.

~~~~~~~~~~~~~~~~

THE GREEN LIFE TREE

My mother couldn't give enough,
My mother gave it free,
My mother nursed the sapling love,
To make of it a tree.
My mother watched the tree grow strong,
And there within its shade,
Where heart and soul and mind belong,
Our family was made.

My father knew a world of pain,
My father kept it hid.
My father walks through hearts again,
Just like he always did.
My father's tears were long unshed,
He never wept for me,
- Save in that brass framed marriage bed,
Where none but she could see.

My father and my mother cared,
This heart of mine speaks true,
And though my father wasn't spared,
He loved his whole life through.
From both of them to all of us,
Comes that which has no name,
The gift of joy from hearts that trust,
- No sweeter present came.

And we their children owe to them,
The green the life tree is,
The buds of hope, the strong, straight stem,
Dew, from a mother's kiss.
Toward the sunlight, thrusting high,
From roots enriched by tears,
Our branches go to touch the sky,
Through happy, golden years.

My mother couldn't give enough,
My mother gave it free.
My father planted seeds of love,
To grow a green life tree.
Both parents watched the tree grow strong,
And there within its shade,
Where riches of the soul belong,
Our family was made.

~~~~~~~~~~~~~~~

WHITE LILIES ON MY HEAD

I caught the 'flu the other day,
The rain was wet, the sky was grey.
My feet were numb, my nose was red
And sneezes shook my fevered head.
I took some Aspros and Night Nurse,
The more I took the pain grew worse.
My legs were weak, my eyes did weep,
I went to bed but couldn't sleep.
My wife made lemon drinks for me,
Blackcurrant juice and cups of tea,
Rubbed jars of Vick into my chest,
I speak the truth, I smelt not fresh.
I used inhalant that was foul,
Raised lumps like eggs on cheek and jowl.
Drank noxious potions of bright hue
Until my bladder swollen grew.
My children stayed away from me,
I blamed them not but let them be,
For how could tender youngsters cling
To such a vile repulsive thing.
I rotted slowly as time passed,
The end seemed near, I couldn't last.
I couldn't see, I couldn't think
But heavens above how I did stink!
I ceased to breathe, great tears were shed,
The doctor came, pronounced me dead.
They laid me out upon a slab.
"Tut, tut!" they cried, and "Oh poor dab!"
My Aunty Blod was quite put out,
I'd borrowed cash and paid back nowt.
She shrieked and wailed and banged her head,
"There's grief for you!" the mourners said.
My suit was promised to our John,
But being cold quite stiff I'd gone.
"Go limp! our Dai" he sadly cried,
"No good to wear it now you've died!"
And turning me upon my face
Removed the suit in frantic haste.
My boots were old and caked with grit
From twenty years worn down the pit.
But cousin Will who nothing spurned
Took both boots off when backs were turned.

My shirt departed from my form
Purloined at speed by uncle Norm,
While combinations full of holes
The village undertaker stole.
With no clothes left to grace my flesh
I lay there in my tenderness.
Whilst many a maiden, sweet and shy
Looked down on me and dropped a sigh.
About this time my coma passed
And watching mourners stood aghast
As I awoke alive and well,
Not up in heaven or down in hell,
But here bereft of winding sheet
In thirty-five Bethesda Street.
Well consternation reigned supreme
And my good wife turned duck-egg green.
"There's mean you are our Dai" she said,
"Quite rich I was when you were dead,
Eight hundred pounds I got from Dan
Our friendly Pearl Insurance man,
Now I will have to give it back,
Pawn all my mourning, all my black,
How could you make me look so small,
You never think of me at all!"
My relatives were all quite mad,
They couldn't keep the clothes they'd had.
They cursed my name, but Aunty Blod
Said, "Glory be and thanks to God,
Perhaps I'll get back on the nose
Every cent the flamer owes!"
Not liking all this frantic fuss
I dressed myself and caught a bus,
And just to please my next of kin
Went to my grave and dived right in.
And there I lie right to this day,
Quite out of sight, not in the way,
And when my good wife visits me
With sandwiches and cups of tea,
Because the world now thinks me dead
She throws white lilies on my head
And sheds fresh tears my grave upon
For her insurance money's gone.
Still all in all I can't complain,
This coffin lid keeps off the rain.

And it's not cold down in this hole
For I have struck a seam of coal
To make great fires deep underground
From six-foot boxes I have found.
And on great handles made of brass
Make stacks of toast to break my fast.
So if on this you'd like to fit
A moral full of poignant wit
Then it must be that to your wife
You're worth more perished than in life,
And though these flames might look like hell
It's heaven on earth where I now dwell!

~~~~~~~~~~~~~~~~~~~~~

CHILDRENS' HOSPITAL

A child on the ward was crying, as visiting parents arrived,
A clock on the wall was ticking, an angel of mercy sighed,
A rocking horse, brilliantly coloured, was host to a dying boy,
As I sat on a bed of sorrow, to witness the passing of joy.

Yet children ran to their parents, smiling or laughing out loud,
Happy and raining sweet kisses on all of the incoming crowd.
Their faces were joyously radiant, they seemed to be brimming with zest,
And though leukaemia had claimed them, no-one would ever have guessed.

Nurses were filling tall vases, with fragrant, fresh floral bouquets,
Grown in an unseen garden, light years from a sick child's gaze.
Cells by the million were dying, in veins that were dry dust streams,
As children rejected their symptoms, and lived to be old in their dreams.

A climbing frame rose in a corner, a wendyhouse stood by the door,
Soft cuddly toys by the armful, were scattered all over the floor.
Babies, devoid of their tresses, were playing with mobiles and such.
Surrounded by worrying parents, who cared for each infant so much.

A clown in a threadbare costume, did somersaults over a chair,
A conjurer, primed with his magic, pulled silver coins out of the air.
Their audience cried out in amazement, enchantment was given out free,
As their faces reflected their rapture, and shone like a beacon on me.

Doctors with charts at the ready, were trying to set minds at ease,
Explaining to folk in the simplest terms, the way they were fighting disease.
Orderlies wheeled sleeping infants, where bone marrow transplants were done,
As I murmured a prayer to the Father, to heal in the name of the Son.

The view through the window was gloomy, the day was in pawn to the night,
Yet hope in young hearts was burning, for stars in their eyes were bright.
They knew every moment was precious, so rode every day on the flood,
To give of themselves in abundance, as cancer diluted their blood.

A child in the ward was singing, as homeward the visitors filed,
A clock on the wall was ticking, an angel of mercy smiled.
A rocking horse, harnessed and ready, was host to a brave young girl,
As I wrapped up the love on offer, and gave it with joy to the world!

~~~~~~~~~~~~~~~~~~~~~~

GOODNESS AND MERCY

Adapted from the 23rd Psalm

The Lord has long my Shepherd been,
There is no greater friend.
He walks with me on meadows green
Where life can have no end.
He shows to me His quiet place,
My spirit doth He hold,
As water from His well of grace
Restores again my soul.

By His example am I shown
The one straight path through life,
That I might in men's hearts enthrone
The glorious name of Christ.
And I will walk in righteousness,
For as He guideth me,
I lose my cloak of sinfulness
As mercy sets me free.

Though I traverse death's shadowed vales,
No evil will I fear,
For this world's final ambush fails
Whilst my dear Lord is near.

His staff of comfort will I take,
His rod of truth I'll touch,
And hell's foundations I will shake,
For He still loves me much.

Before my enemies He stands
A table to set forth,
Provisioned by His loving hands
From Heaven's eternal source.
And fed from this my strength returns
To gird my armour on,
For where the flame of glory burns,
The faithful heart is strong.

My head with oil He gently bathes,
He stoops my feet to wash,
And my immortal soul He saves
By death upon a cross.
My cup of joy now overflows,
And on its blessed flood,
My salvaged spirit Heavenward goes
Through His redeeming blood.

Goodness and mercy follow me,
Not only on this day,
But through all future time to be
Whilst at my side He stays.
And I within His house will dwell
Content to see his face
Rejoicing I was kept from hell
By His amazing grace!

~~~~~~~~~~~~~~~~~~~~~

THE SHADE REGRET

Never paint the shade regret
On any passing day
For life is brief, and man's belief
Is but a touch away.
Renew your brush with evening's hush,
A blend of twilight themes,
Where sunset's red is put to bed
With gold, enchanted, dreams.

Never speak an unkind word
For these will still defame,
And echo on when life has gone,
To poison memory's name.
So think again, before the pain
Your wounding words have wrought
Has reached that stage, beyond old age,
Where kindness can't be bought.

Never give your heart until
You're sure the taker knows
This gift of love is strong enough
To harvest seed it sows.
We only part with loving hearts
But once 'till life grows cold,
And when this breaks, the grief it makes
Will fester in the soul.

Always do what's right and good,
The very best you can,
Then light and truth will last through youth,
And you'll become a man.
This planet earth awaits rebirth
And this your strength can do;
Walk tall and straight through childhood's gate,
This moment waits for you!

~~~~~~~~~~~~~~~~~

LIFTED HER UP WITH MY SOUL

In memory of a beloved lost daughter

"Lift me up, oh! lift me up, please daddy raise me up high,
There's folk in front, and I want to see the gala procession go by.
I want to look at coloured floats, and clowns in costumes of gold."
So I lifted her up, this daughter of mine, I lifted her up with my soul.

"Don't ever leave me, daddy" she said, as we followed the marching bands.
I bent to kiss her cherry-red lips, and cradled her face in my hands.
"I'm with you forever" I whispered to her, "and never apart we'll be,
For you are the gem in the crown of my life, and worlds without end to me."

"Take me and keep me, daddy" said she, as the term of my marriage broke down.
"I don't want to go too far from your arms, or live in a distant town."
I promised her all that she wanted to hear, and I tried not to break that vow,
But time and events conspired against me and there's no-one to promise to now.

"Please come and see me, daddy" she wrote, "for I miss you so very much.
I long for your smile, I long for your warmth, and I ache just to feel your touch."
So down through the years I visited her, and left her each time in pain,
And it comes to me now with a stab at the heart, that I'll never see her again.

"Wait for me darling" I nightly pray, for her Saviour has carried her home.
In the flood of her years, with so much to do, she has gone and left me alone.
And though she was married, with daughter and son, the love that we shared
was so deep,
I still hear her voice in the full of the day, and hear it again in my sleep.

"Lift me up" I hear her say, "please daddy, raise me on high.
There's angels in front, and I want to see God's gala procession pass by.
I just want to ask him to save you a place, that later we both could share."
So I lifted her up, this daughter of mine, and raised her to Jesus in prayer.

Yes, over the heads of angels she rose, as the glorious vision appeared
A King whose head was crowned by thorns, and hands by nails are pierced.
A million stars shone from His face, His cloak was of burnished gold
As I held her in love, with the power of faith, and lifted her up with my soul!

~~~~~~~~~~~~~~~~~

WHERE ELSE COULD LOVE EMBRACE YOU

Dancing, forever dancing, brings joy into our lives,
As social evenings make the hours sublime.
We look around the ballroom floor at husbands and their wives,
Who pirouette until the end of time.

Where else could love embrace you, or music charm your ears,
What else could weave the strands of true romance?
Where all the warmest feelings, the laughter and the tears,
Come flowing from the magic of the dance.

We are the heirs of movement, the children of an art
That through the years has made the spirit soar.
Demolished social barriers and torn class veils apart,
As gracefully we glide across the floor.

We hear the same sweet music, and sing the songs of old,
Which bring so many memories from the past.
Where happy times remembered, when all the world was gold,
Are echoes of a childhood that will last.

We have great social evenings with leaders whom we love,
And those who all sustain us in the break.
Unselfishly they work for us, and when the goings rough,
They smooth our path with all the pains they take.

We spare a thought for others too, who gave more than they took,
For each of these was more than 'just a friend',
And all the lovely people who are in life's golden book,
Who cared so much and served us to the end.

We've shared so much together, the joy, the grief, the pain,
And know that troubles shared are troubles halved.
We talk about our childrens lives and reminisce again
About their funny ways that made us laugh.

We're all prepared to listen to the stories people tell,
The little things that make our lives worthwhile.
Then dance around in pleasure with the folk we know so well,
While basking in the sunshine of a smile.

Sequence clubs are made of this, and whilst the world looks on,
The values that we hold all seem to glow.
Nothing changes in our hearts, the good is never gone,
In all of us deep friendship seems to grow.
People too, are all concern, for others not themselves,
In every soul compassion is a flower;
And in each corner of the mind, where trust and honour dwell,
Then thought is always master of the hour.

Dancing is a way of life, what else could take its place?
There is no other pastime half as good.
Each intricate manoeuvre, is a movement full of grace,
When sequences are fully understood.

We may falter, we may stumble, but with dancers who are friends
We are led out of our troubles so it seems,
To swing, cha cha and rumba, even foxtrot now and then
As we dance into the sunset of our dreams!

~~~~~~~~~~~~~~~~~~~~~~~

THE BIGGEST FOOL

I couldn't find my spectacles, I really panicked then,
For how could I see where I was, if they weren't found again.
How could I know how dark it was, or if there was some light,
If I couldn't find my spectacles and so regain my sight.

I blundered round the living room and opened every drawer,
Cut my fingers on sharp things, like pins I never saw.
Fell backwards over curled up rugs and sat upon the floor,
Where my dear wife then trod on me, as she came through the door.

"What are you looking for" she cried, "and why this pain and grief?
The awful noise you're making, dear, is quite beyond belief.
I thought it was an elephant, demolishing the bricks,
And not the father of my child who weights but eight stone six!"

'Twas then I told her of my plight, the spectacles I'd lost,
The awful dark that made me blind, the money they had cost.
She laughed so much she wet herself, and looked a perfect wreck,
As pointing here, below my chin, she said "they're on your neck!"

And sure enough, that's where they were, tied to a length of tape.
Around my neck, and on my throat, where they could not escape,
And I, who feared eternal dark had come to blindfold me
Was made to look the biggest fool, that ever you did see!

~~~~~~~~~~~~~~~~~~~~~~~

WHEN WICK WAS LIT

I saw life's candle slowly burn
Until the last wax ran.
And when its molten flow had ceased
I knew creation's plan.
For I was there when wick was lit
And my eyes first saw light,
To know the love of seventy years
Before an endless night.
I felt my mother's wondrous love
As I was early fed.
Took suck from her and comfort too,
As she lay in her bed.
Not knowing that the pain she faced
While troubled years unwound,
Would carry her to that damp grave,
In Cefn, underground.

I watch again from time's high hill
The house where I was born.
Its tiny rooms, museums now,
Where childhood weeps forlorn.
O! was it yesterday I stood
Within those walls of joy,
To feel the future lure me on,
When I was yet a boy.

I see once more the map of age
Upon my father's face.
The continents of hope and trust
The seas of endless grace.
The granite highways driving through
The darkness pain affords,
For he was every shining lamp
Upon those twisting roads.

I mourn for every value lost,
And each great truth that dies.
For honour brought to deep disgrace,
For truth transformed to lies.
For every child who begs for bread,
For people, war has slain.
As mindlessly we murder love
For those who still remain.

I see life's candle burn until
Its wax becomes a stream,
That fiery pours into the mind
To scar each youthful dream.
And though I watched when wick was lit
And knew creation's plan
I wish that God used better tools
When He created man!

~~~~~~~~~~~~~~~~~

R.I.P.

Dear mother and friend, brave unto death,
    Uncomplaining and sweet to the very last breath.
Why should we mourn you, now that you've passed,
    To a place that is rest and a peace that will last.

THE FULLNESS OF TIME

Remember the journeys we made in our youth,
In those dirty old trains that shook every tooth?
The sad, mournful whistles, the mountains of dust,
The ruptured coach springs with their coating of rust.
The window straps flapping on stained carriage doors,
Fag ends that wriggled on black, filthy floors.
And always the clackety, clickety, clack,
Of stuttering wheels on their riveted track
That made us sing songs to their rhythm and rhyme,
As we thundered non stop round the contours of time.

Remember the Sunday School outings of yore,
From stations that simply aren't there anymore.
Packed in a train like a can of sardines
By Sunday School teachers without any means.
With Watcyn, our minister, checking his watch,
And Jonas (The Hill) with his bottle of Scotch,
Who drank like a fish to the clickety clack
Of wheels that stammered all over the track.
And children would chant to their rhythm and rhyme
As we rolled to the sea through that valley of mine.

Remember our wonder as Barry drew near,
We kids sniffed the sea and our fathers the beer.
Mothers and grannies all wetted their lips,
Inhaling the bouquet of fried fish and chips.
We rolled to a stop and the doors opened wide,
And we burst from that train like an incoming tide.
For the clickety, clackety, clicketty, clack,
Echoed no more from the wheels or the track,
And no-one could measure our feelings sublime
As we raced to the beach in that moment of time.

Remember, remember the anguish and pain
We felt as we all travelled homeward again?
With skin badly burned and stings from the bees,
Bruises and swellings and grazes on knees.
And O! what a nightmare as stations flashed by,
And grit from the steam came and lodged in the eye.
To the clicketty, clackety, clicketty, clack,
Of the musical wheels on the thundering track;
And tears would be shed to the rhythm and rhyme
As crying we came to the end of the line.

Remember that parents are children grown old.
When young we were silver, in age we are gold.
From Great Western stations we'll no more depart,
But memories they gave us are stored in the heart.
And yet from the flames that once burned in the past,
The boilers are lit and the pistons drive fast,
And the clicketty, clackety, clicketty clack
Comes alive in our dreams from yesterday's track.
As singing we go to the rhythm and rhyme
To the place that is rest, in the fullness of time.

~~~~~~~~~~~~~~~~~~~~~~

DYLAN THOMAS

Dylan Thomas was a gift to mankind,
A spool of great verse that would swiftly unwind.
Magnificent words, unmatched by his peers,
That shook you with mirth, or drowned you in tears.

His stature was such, if you mentioned his name,
He was seen as a giant, perceived as a flame,
That burned all his listeners like fiery coal,
To melt all the ice that formed in the soul.

His Wales was surrealist, peopled by folk
Entranced or tormented by words that he spoke.
His valleys were chasms, his mountains so high,
Their peaks were obscured by clouds in his sky.

From Swansea to London, L.A to New York,
His mind floated free on great rivers of talk.
Spellbound, folk listened to rapturous rhyme,
That echoes forever down reaches of time.

We'll never quite know what he meant by his words,
For he soared in the sky of his dreams like a bird.
But the song that he sang to the beat of his wings,
Is the same that the soul of a nightingale sings.

Yes, Dylan was gifted by God to this earth.
Wales was his cradle, and mighty his birth.
His verse still exalts us, and somehow it seems,
The book of his life comes alive in our dreams.

~~~~~~~~~~~~~~~~~~~~~~

THE ROSE OF MONTREUX

We flew on a plane and travelled by train
To the beautiful town of Montreux,
Where roads that we take sweep down to the lake,
And flowers of paradise grow.
The steamers cruise by with a klaxon horn cry,
As people all wave to the shore.
And the joy in the soul, as such beauty unfolds
Will live in our hearts evermore.

The railway trains climb to a summit sublime,
A place where our dreams are reborn.
Where the air is so sweet and the chalets so neat,
They seem to make peace with the dawn.
While the bells on the cows, as the meadows they browse
Re-echo and ring as they twirl,
And the stations flash by on mountains so high
They look like the roof of the world.

Our thoughts still move on to Chateau Chillon,
The fortress that seems to embrace
The best and the worst of Lord Byron's verse,
Though its walls wear a gloomier face.
Villeneuve waits with its terraced estates
In a bay that is stroked by the breeze.
And hang gliders land on the promenade strand
To frighten the birds from the trees.

The Funiculaire rides up the fir clad hillsides,
Where Glion is second to none.
And the day is so fresh, it catches your breath,
Then turns it to mist in the sun.
The vista expands where the little church stands,
As we look from the balcony rail
Of that lovely cafe where time passed away
Like a beautiful fairy tale.

We came to Lausanne when Monday began,
And walked to the lake down the hill.
Had tea quite supreme, and a mango ice-cream,
As all thirsty travellers will.
Then sat on a bench and listened to French
That was spoken by folk by the score,
And were lulled into sleep on the Pedalo beach
By the waves as they sang to the shore.

The best day we had was our trip to Gstaad,
When June wore her best summer dress.
A lift to the stars in the luxury cars
Of the blue Panoramic Express.
The mountains stood proud where the Alps kissed the clouds,
The snow on their peaks dazzling white.
And we left with regret, what we'll never forget,
A truly magnificent sight.

One day we'll return, where our memories burn,
To the furnace of joy that's Montreux.
Where the rose of the town in its delicate grown
Will nod as we pass by the shore.
And the little cafes with their lights all ablaze
Will welcome us back to the fold,
As we travel in grace through this wonderful place
Where dreamers will never grow old!

~~~~~~~~~~~~~~~~~~~~~~

SHE IS MY WIFE

She is alive with joy, and wears a cloak of charm,
Her body soft to touch, her lips inviting, warm.
Her love surrounds my soul, and like a king I
Sit enthroned amongst the stars, within the palace of the sky.

She is the voice of Spring, the dewy freshness of the dawn.
She's like the winds that pass and yet are never gone.
Divinity is she, the very essence of my life,
She is the beating heart in me, she is my wife!

~~~~~~~~~~~~~~~~~~~~~~

BRIGHT BUTTERFLIES

How can they pin bright butterflies to polished boards of wood?
What inner urge this satisfies I've never understood.
To me, a creature of such grace should float up in the sky,
And not end up in some glass case, too dead to please the eye.

How dare they cripple elephants for just two ivory tusks;
And leave these beasts the eye enchants to die there in the dust?
The greed in man is beyond belief, for when these beasts have gone,
Then all our tears and all our grief won't see their kind live on.

Why should we let great highways race through fields that once were green,
Or see rain forests laid to waste to make this world unclean.
We poison everything we touch, we foul the once pure streams;
And as man's brightest hopes we crush, we tarnish all our dreams.

Perhaps quite soon this world will die, then burn up in the sun.
And there'll be none to question why, how this was first begun.
And cases of bright butterflies, with elephants destroyed,
Will mingle with the fallen trees, and perish in the void!

~~~~~~~~~~~~~~~~~~~~~~

A BAND OF SOLID GOLD

O! Granny how I loved you, so very long ago,
When we all lived in Darren View, where once you watched me grow.
When we were close in faith and thought, when we both went to church,
Where we sang hymns in harmony, as our two voices merged.

How glorious was our friendship, a blend of young and old,
A thread of youthful silver on a band of solid gold.
We didn't have to speak our love, we felt it everywhere,
She saw it shining in my eyes, with hers reflected there.

We played those lovely games of cards, the hours did seem to spin,
Endless hands of knockout whist, she always seemed to win.
Her glasses would slide down her nose, her eyes would be revealed,
And happiness would shine from them, for joy can't be concealed.

We sometimes stood in silence and shared a wordless prayer,
And surely He who graced a cross was also standing there;
For granny was a friend of His, and walked close by His side,
And took from Him that priceless gift, the love that never died.

O Granny! how I loved you, those days before the war,
Before the sickness and the pain, and all the grief you saw.
And I will go on loving you, until in Heaven we meet,
When we'll sing songs in harmony, with angel voices sweet!

~~~~~~~~~~~~~~~~~~~~~~

THE MARATHON

I don't think I'll run in the marathon,
I'm feeling too shaky you see.
For I have got problems so major,
They frighten the life out of me.
My waterworks sometimes malfunction,
My hernia was never much fun.
My teeth are so false, they always fall out,
Each time that I go for a run.

I filled in my entry and sent it,
(I felt really strong at the time)
Believed in myself as a sportsman,
Regarded my style as sublime.
Never thought that my fractured pelvis,
Or the multiple growth of my piles,
Would be such a terrible hindrance
To running the twentysix miles.

The surgical stockings I'm wearing,
Obscure my varicose veins.
My knees are a prey to arthritis,
I'll never see seventy again.
I've started to wear contact lenses,
Because when I sneeze or I cough,
My ears tend to wiggle so badly,
My spectacles tend to drop off.

These shoulders of mine are both frozen,
Much colder than New Zealand lamb.
I've managed to get tennis elbow
Through eating too much strawberry jam.
Both hips are now ripe for replacement,
My liver's at war with my spleen,
And so colour blind are my kidneys,
The water I'm passing is green.

I ran up the stairs just this morning,
(You have to, to get to our loo).
Lost most of my breath on the landing,
As elderly athletes will do.
The spray that I use for my asthma,
I shot by mistake in my eye.
So blinded and breathless I stumbled
Convinced I was going to die.

I don't think the Marathon suits me,
I'm better at twenty yard sprints.
Anything further quite daunts me,
My legs always end up in splints.
As I settle myself in this wheelchair,
And violent activity shun,
I'll watch the damn race on the telly,
It's better than having to run!

~~~~~~~~~~~~~~~~~~~~~~~

THE LITTLE BOY I USED TO BE

I saw a fearsome sight today,
That turned each hair of mine to grey.
For in a looking glass nearby,
I saw myself fall down and die.

I rushed to look into the glass
To see the future and the past,
The little boy I used to be
Look down upon this end of me.

He stared in wonder and alarm,
As if my corpse could do him harm.
Then knelt and held my hand in his,
And on my lips bestowed a kiss.

And lo! a wondrous thing occurred,
For my soul, flying like a bird,
Left prostrate form, and merged into
The little boy that once I knew.

This was a magic, golden, blend,
For now I knew life didn't end,
But turned again upon itself
To come full circle like all else.

One day I'll know what all this means,
But just for now my waking dreams
Are haunted by what came to pass
When I looked in that mirrored glass.

~~~~~~~~~~~~~~~~~~~~~~~

THE BEST OF US

Edna was more than a sister to me,
For I'll swear we shared the same heart,
Thought the same thoughts, did the same things
Though we lived such a distance apart.
Worshipped our God in the very same way,
And she would be smiling at me,
As I preached to her friends in the Market Square Church,
For none were more faithful than she.

Edna was never a burden to me,
For I know that she lifted my soul,
Made me feel young in the rot of my days,
For dreamers will never grow old.
She loved all the words that were born in my mind,
The poems she helped to inspire,
And she could recite every line that I wrote,
As if it came straight from the fire.

Edna was dearer by far to me
Than all the queens of this earth;
And I will proclaim to my dying day
That her blood was royal from birth.
Others came first every day of her life,
A ministering angel was she,
For she tended the sick and cared for the old,
And she gave of her services free.

Edna was autumn, summer and spring,
With never a sprinkling of frost.
Winter would melt in the warmth of her faith,
Which came from a Man on a cross.
She lived every moment of every long day,
Sharing with those she adored
The simplest of pleasures no money can buy,
But only the best can afford.

Edna was mother to daughter and sons
And she was a wonderful wife,
So they will remember the joy that she gave
Every hour and day of her life.
None can replace her for she was unique,
A jewel so priceless and rare
That it sparkles and glows on the breast of their love,
As it did in the crown of her hair.

O! Edna, my sister, you'll not be forgot,
For you were the best of us all.
Plucked from our midst when the last trumpet blew,
For you had to respond to that call.
The great reaper came with his angelic host
When the ears of your corn were ripe,
And gathered you in with the true and the blest,
The most wonderful harvest of Christ.

So I, as your brother, will stay part of you
For we grew from the very same seed,
Had the same father, loved the same mam,
And turned to them both in our need.
Protected each other when stormy days came,
Who knew when the lightening would strike?
Walked through the darkness of old Merthyr town
In good and bad times alike.

Edna was sister and comfort to me,
And her heart will continue to beat
Whilst I think the same thoughts, do the same things
That made our living so sweet.
The God we both worship holds her in His hand,
And I'm sure she's still smiling at me
In the way that she did in that Market Square Church,
For none were more loving than she!

~~~~~~~~~~~~~~~~

JOB EXPERIENCE

I little thought so long ago, that I'd grow old one day.
My life just seemed forever spring, with winter far away.
I felt I was immortal then, there seemed no end to joy,
Yet looking back across the years, I'm still that same small boy.

Perhaps it's better in our youth if we are never told
The changes that the years can bring, as wein turn grow old.
A seed will grow into a flower, that one day soon will die.
Its petals all, will fade and fall, and on earth's bosom lie.

Some children in this modern age, think we are past our best.
Poke fun at us, and even mug, old pensioners at rest.
Yet we fought two world wars for them, and kept this country free,
And memories of comrades dead, still draws the tears from me.

We don't feel different from the young, we hold the common view,
We're made to feel we're second hand, whilst they themselves are new.
Yet we were children in our turn and they will one day find,
Advancing years can bring you peace, and even make you kind.

I'm seventy-six, and feel eighteen, my future still looks bright.
I take my wife to sequence clubs and dance into the night.
I meet grandchildren fresh from school, and shop three times a week.
Yet still find time to write this verse, and to an audience speak.

Perhaps this job experience lark is just what old folk need.
There are new challenges to face, as each great cause we plead.
And surely all the wisdom gained, can be passed on in turn,
If only those who mock us now, will find the time to learn!

~~~~~~~~~~~~~~~~~~~~~~~

LITTLE CHILDREN

Little children are the future,
We must guide them on their way,
Monitor each thought and movement,
See them safely through each day.
Keep drug pushers from their presence,
See no paedophile draws near.
Let them grow into fine people
Who will hold their honour dear.

Once there was no need to watch them
For the world was safer then.
Children could relate to adults,
Even see each one as friend.
Streets and parks were full of youngsters,
Outdoor spaces ripe with joy.
How I wish that I could take them
Back to where I was a boy.

Mountainsides were realms of pleasure,
Where we all could safely roam.
Active evenings in the chapel,
Love and kindness in the home.
In the towns no busy traffic,
So we played down quiet roads,
With the air so unpolluted
We could see the stars blaze forth.

We were free from mindless violence,
Television was unknown.
We would sit entranced in parlours
Listening to the gramophone.
Marvellous tenors lit our darkness,
Bass profundos sang their roles,
Great sopranos touched our heart strings,
Gold contraltos warmed our souls.

Cinemas were hall of gladness,
Pleasure just within our means.
Images that flickered madly
On long faded silver screens.
Crunching monster mint imperials,
Sucking sherbert through a straw,
Sitting there in friendly darkness,
Wrapped up in the films we saw.

Sisters, brothers, grown-up cousins,
Took great care of every child.
Seeing they were unmolested,
That their lives were undefiled.
Innocence was theirs to treasure,
This rich gift was theirs to keep,
Now it lies in trust forever,
Where the saints and angels sleep.

Little children are the future,
We must see them safely through
Tender childhood, adolescence,
Make their paths straight and true.
Keep abusers from their presence,
Lead them to a brighter dawn,
Where they too can be examples
To the children yet unborn!

~~~~~~~~~~~~~~~~

IS IT TRUE?

Do we feel we're that much older than we did when we were young?
I don't mean in the body, in the heart or in the lung.
But somewhere deep inside us where the soul and spirit meet,
And the magic that is living makes each moment fresh and sweet.

When we look into a mirror is it age we really see?
Or is it someone from the past who looks like you and me?
Someone younger than the springtime, someone fresher than the dawn,
Who never looks past summer to a winter's frosty morn.

Is it true that we're now wrinkled and our skin has lost its sheen?
That hair and teeth are missing and there's gaps where they have been.
Can we accept that childhoods gone, or do we look instead,
To that dear place where hope still lives, and dreams are never dead.

Yet beauty doesn't dwell alone upon a young girl's skin,
For as she grows into old age, she's still beautiful within.
And there is someone who made us unto His image born,
Who sees us as we really are when youth and looks have gone!

~~~~~~~~~~~~~~~~~~~~

AND LAUGH ALL THE WAY TO THE GRAVE

Cardiff's a home for all nations,
Carmarthen's a place for the Welsh,
Swansea with all its privations,
Is much better off than ourselves.
For we are the folk from the valleys,
Where men spend their lives on the dole,
As pits are set up as Aunt Sallys
And knocked off their perch by King Coal.

Newport's a new border borough,
Bridgend is a feeble man's joke,
Brecon's a field with a furrow,
And Neath is a town without hope.
But what of the people of Maerdy,
Of Merthyr and grey Aberdare,
They don't sip their iced rum Bacardis
Or dance like a Welsh Fred Astaire.

Aberystwyth is seaside and leisure,
Porthcawl is a wet windy day,
Caerphilly is castle and pleasure,
Llanelli is rugby at play.
Yet up in Pontlottyn and Bargoed,
Tredegar and dark Ebbw Vale,
You won't hear the stock prices argued,
They're putting their homes up for sale!

Builth Wells is just waiting for heaven,
Llandudno is next in the queue,
Chepstow's a bridge on the Severn,
Cwmbran's unbelievably new.
But pop up to drab Abercynon,
Treharris or sad Ynysfach,
You won't see their unemployed running,
Except to a bench in the park.

Wales is a map without features,
Aggravating in so many ways.
It exports to England its teachers,
And keeps we poor Welsh in our place.
With pits that are uneconomic,
With steelworks that no-one can save,
Perhaps we should all buy a comic
And laugh all the way to the grave!

~~~~~~~~~~~~~~~~~

YOU ASK ME

(To my wife)

You ask me if I need you, as if this doesn't show.
You ask me if I love you, as if you didn't know.
You hunger to be wanted, as if this couldn't be.
O! lovely one, don't you yet know, that you are all to me.

I ask you if you need me, for words are not your strength.
I ask how much you love me, the height, the breadth, the length.
I want this sweet assurance, though you are much too shy
To voice the feelings that you hide as life slips swiftly by.

So let us both be open, and each declare our love.
To show ourselves and all the world, that we still care enough.
Then hunger will be satisfied, for who will want again,
When words and feelings join as one, and joy replaces pain.

~~~~~~~~~~~

THIS OLD MOUNTAIN

I have sat on this old mountain,
Through ten thousand nights and days,
Felt the silence, heard the shouting,
Watched my world and all its ways.
Through it all my heart is singing,
'Til past joy I reach that place,
Where my gift of thanks I'm bringing,
There before that throne of grace.

I have kissed a hundred lasses,
Looked them all straight in the eye.
Told each one that though love passes,
While it lasts the bright sparks fly.
I have gathered life's dear harvest,
Stored my grain where no man steals,
Held the sweetest, kept the fairest,
Crushed bad seeds beneath my heels.

Through the seasons, I have squandered
Those rich gifts that I've received.
Through time's valleys I have wandered,
Through black days my heart has grieved.
But the balance at the ending,
Tips the scales firm on my side,
Now in age, through hope, I'm mending,
Dreams I broke in foolish pride.

There below, with sunshine fading,
Shadows fall from hills above.
Dear friends homes that I have stayed in,
Light with joy from flames of love.
There the lovely, golden, past walks,
Hand in hand with what's to be,
And the one I loved at last talks,
From the vaults of memory.

I have sat on this old mountain,
Off, and on, through all of my days.
Drank of life's eternal fountain,
Watched my world and all its ways.
Through it all in joy and sadness,
I go forward to that place,
Where I'll lay bright gifts of gladness,
There before that throne of grace.

~~~~~~~~~~~~~~~~

SO HELPLESS

I am a tiny baby, too weak to have my say,
So I lie helpless in this cot to scream and cry all day.
They must be callous blighters, perhaps they're both stone deaf,
Or they would know my nappy's full, and I don't smell too fresh.

I suffer from the colic, or so the doctor said.
The wind is trapped behind my heart, each time that I am fed.
If they don't come and pick me up, and burp me pretty quick,
The wind will blow me inside out, and then I <u>will</u> be sick!

It's hard to be so helpless, and grownups quite forget
That they were fragile infants once and easily upset.
I <u>need</u> my feeds to be on time, to me it's only right,
Yet parents are a tired lot who want to sleep all night.

I'm much too young to train them, perhaps a prayer would help,
I'm certain God is on my side, I can't do much myself.
A miracle is what I need if I am not to die,
Some talc to soothe my private parts, a nappy, warm and dry.

I'll hold my breath to frighten them, I'll make my face go blue.
I'll fake an epileptic fit, as naughty children do.
I'll pull my hair out by its roots and then resort to tears,
And if all this they just ignore, I'll wiggle both my ears!

Yet though I weigh a few scant pounds, the power I wield is vast,
For I've bequeathed disarming traits, from babies in the past.
I only have to lift my hand and squeeze each finger tight,
To turn them into mindless fools, for they're not all that bright.

So here I lie in this small cot, prepared to entertain.
To gurgle like an idiot child, who's born with half a brain.
I am the centre of their lives, the hub 'round which they spin,
And callous blighters though they are, they're still quite soft within!

~~~~~~~~~~~~~~~~~~~~~~~

MY CROP

Now that my days are numbered,
This thought with you I leave.
Why do we live so short a time
From when we were a seed?
Some trees will grow forever,
The sun outlasts the sky.
Yet my crop will be harvested
When forth I go to die!

~~~~~~~~~~~~~~~~~

WHERE OUR MAKER HAS BEEN

I saw the sun jump over a hill
I thought it displayed considerable skill
By missing the trees that grew on its crest
And leaving the birds asleep in their nests.

I watched the moon dive under a cloud,
"Full marks for that," I shouted aloud,
For not one fluff of that cumulous mass
Did the moon disturb as I watched it pass.

I saw some stars in the Milky Way
Lose all their sparkle and turn to grey;
And hoped the giver of joy and pain
Would make them twinkle for me again.

I felt the breeze caressing my skin,
It shot up my sleeve and bounced off my chin.
"Great Scott!" I exclaimed, "what a zephyr that is!"
As it tickled my fancy and blew me a kiss.

I couldn't help thinking that this was planned,
The sky, the earth, the sea and the sand.
Before they were formed then nothing was there
Not even the dawn or the midnight air.

For sun, moon and stars, with breezes that blow
Are part of creation I'll have you know.
They warm and they shine and wash the world clean
So we can all see where our Maker has been!

~~~~

THIS IS THE STREET

This is the street into which I was born,
In the summer heat of a late June morn.
Just thirty-nine houses on either side,
A hundred yards long and twenty feet wide.
With every front door direct to the street,
And every front doorstep scrubbed, polished and neat.
And it lay in the valley in which we dwell,
At the top of the hill with a brewery smell.

The Council had named it Darren View
With tongue in cheek, for everyone knew
The view of the Darren was ugly and bare,
Back to back houses for families to share.
With hordes of children in every street,
Great hulking brutes and babes on the teat,
Deafening the valley in which we dwell
By their steady din and occasional yell.

And the siege of our house on pension day
By Lisa Richards and Hannah Day.
By Mother Auger and Widow Jones
And Dai Small Coal of the wheedling tones.
But this we lend in charities name,
For they and we are flesh of the same
And all of the valley in which we dwell
Is nothing so much as a debtors cell.

And my Gran's contralto, sweet as the dawn,
Like the good Lord blowing His golden horn.
Accompanied by tenors with upward glances
Who pierced the roof with their silvery lances,
As if they could reach with their Hallelujah's
The compassionate heart of the great Jehovah,
Who must hear of the valley in which we dwell
From the voices of heaven, rising from hell.

And my Grandpa Morris, neat and dapper
In a blue serge suit from a pawnshop wrapper.
With his ready smile and his shafts of wit,
And his half an ounce of pigtail twist
That he chewed with relish, without his teeth,
From the corner shop to the pit at Glyn Neath,
Ten miles from the valley in which we dwell
To the four foot seam that he cut so well.

He had worked underground since the age of ten,
And he was to his mates, a prince among men.
His faith was a pint and his church was a pub
While cheese with his bread was succulent grub.
But he carried his drink with a regal air
From his twinkling feet to his thinning hair,
And he graced the valley in which we dwell
From New Year's Day to the First Noel.

And my lovely mam, with her heart of gold,
Who cradled the young and cared for the old.
Who worked at her washtub out on the stones
Till the acids burned right into her bones,
While the black fates laughed and my young heart wept,
As the seasons raced and the poisons crept
From the mists of the valley in which we dwell
To the tender heart that I loved so well.

She was five foot nothing, some would say,
But to me she was everything, everyday,
From the blaze of noon to the black of night
Her love was the torch that burned so bright.
Her voice was the balm that soothed my fears,
Her apron the magic that dried my tears,
And she gave to the valley in which we dwell
The gift of a love that pain couldn't quell.

And what of my father?, a man racked by pain,
Up there on the mountain in snow and in rain.
A man with a vision, a man born to dream,
Up there in the filth of an opencast seam.
A brain set afire from joy in the soul,
Quenched in the depths of a waterlogged hole.
His world was the valley in which we dwell,
No king with an empire could love it so well.

I still see his smile, and I still hear his voice,
The shadows have fled and my heart can rejoice
That I am his son and I shared living hours
That time cannot bury neath crosses and flowers.
O father! My father, your dear face to touch,
You suffered such pain and I loved you so much.
Your past lights the valley in which we dwell,
While the joy that you brought, the heart cannot tell.

Yet there is a lesson we mortals must learn,
The past is a place where our minds can return,
To visit the homes and the people we knew
Our brothers and sisters, our parents so true.
Through sorrow and laughter the vision unfolds,
We live with the dream that the memory holds.
Undying the flame that transfigures the shell
Of the soul of the valley in which we dwell!

~~~~~~~~~~~~~~~~~~~~~~

AS STARS BLAZE FORTH

There is a world inside us that's waiting to be found.
Continents of hope and trust, where myriad joys abound.
It is a place of wonder, it is the birth of Spring,
Where storms no longer thunder, and nightingales still sing.

There is a fairy story, etched deep on every mind,
A tale of endless glory, where folk are always kind.
With children sweet and tender, with homes still warmed by love,
And nights of jewelled splendour, as stars burst forth above.

There is a poignant yearning within this hidden world.
Where beacons are kept burning and flags of hope unfurled.
'Twas placed there by Lord Jesus, as on a cross He hung,
And when we speak He hears us, for He himself was young.

There is a world of feeling, inside the human soul,
And as I pray here, kneeling, it makes my spirit whole.
Of faith is this compounded, on Gospels it is proved,
And here where love abounded, this world can't be removed.

~~~~~~~~~~~~~~~~

CHRISTMAS REVISITED

I sit and think and ask again,
Can Christmas move me still;
With memories of joy and pain
And snow upon the hill?
Must every hour of every year
Be hours the seasons spun,
Or will the Lord of Hosts appear
And say; 'This is my Son!'
Will magic work its own sweet way
Inside the hearts of men?
Will countless pilgrims kneel and pray
In distant Bethlehem?
Can that bright star of long ago,
Light up our darkening sky,
That we might see beyond its glow,
To find the reasons why?
Around us lap the tides of time
That rise from timeless seas,
Where all the years, both yours and mine
Are drowned in memories.
The childlike voices of the poor
That piped the Christmas hymns,
The knock of soft hands on the door
The joy no darkness dims.
My father's dear and smiling face,
With love in every line;
His heart an open caring place,
His joy alive in mine.
The valley wasted while he walked
The high enclosing hills,
But through his spirit Christmas talked,
And I can hear him still.
This is the gift of God to men,
That we must show we care,
And walk with love to Bethlehem
To live our Christmas prayer.
Our hearts were young so long ago
And Mother is a word
That keeps life's springtime all aglow
While yet your voice is heard.

Stay with us brave heart through the years,
We need your tender touch,
That we might say through joy and tears
We love you, Mam, so much.
My pen stops now, but Christmas lives,
The infant child is born.
The mind is cleansed, the heart forgives,
For this is Christmas morn.
Now ring the bells, the shadow lifts,
For God is man this day;
The message burns through cards and gifts,
For Christ has shown the way.

~~~~~~~~~~~~~~~~~~~~~~~

WHEN I CARED TWICE AS MUCH

There isn't much that I can do to change the hearts of men.
There was a time when I tried hard, but I was younger then.
I see a world through jaded eyes, my heart's no longer touched,
And I'm not half the man I was, when I cared twice as much.

It's not the way I started out, back in those far off days.
When every word I spoke rang true, and every song was praise.
My soul was whole, not crippled then, I didn't need a crutch,
For I was twice the man I am, now I care half as much.

I shared the pain of those in need, when I was but a youth.
Locked horns with those who hated change, and fought them hand and tooth.
Took many insults, undeserved, but never bore a grudge,
For I was more than twice a man when I cared oh so much.

Perhaps one day, my heart will melt, and I will once more know,
The driving, caring force of youth that through my veins once flowed.
This then the hope that spurs me on, the only straw I clutch,
Then I won't be just half a man, when I care twice as much.

I don't know when the caring stopped, or why the life force died.
Indifference was the cross I bore, though this I tried to hide.
And though I'm not a man to yearn for rich rewards or such,
I'd like to be the man I was, when I cared twice as much.

Compassion must be nursed and fed, not starved throughout the years.
Joy and laughter, grief and pain, should mingle with the tears.
Then men like me won't stumble past the grief we've left untouched
And we'll be doubly blessed in life, when we care twice as much!

~~~~~~~~~~~~~~~~~~~~~~~

TOO EXCITING

We all seem to need recreation,
A change from the hard working day,
For we are a sport loving nation
Who never mix work with our play.
We nod in our sleep watching cricket,
And shout ourselves hoarse as we see
Grown men kicking balls on the telly,
It's all too exciting for me!

~~~~~~~~~~~~~~~~~

COLD FEET

Cold feet can ruin a marriage
Though snoring will run it quite close.
While wrapping the duvet around you
Is grimmer than picking your nose.
A wife can be pushed to distraction
By slurping your tea as you sup
And almost becomes suicidal
When you leave the toilet seat up.

As inwards you come from the garden,
Without wiping feet on the mat.
Leaves, mud and compost stuck to your heels
And whoopsie from some mangy cat.
Your spouse will be writing instructions
To people who deal with divorce,
For all the nagging she's doing
Is making her terribly hoarse.

When you fail to clean up your bath tub
And the toe-nails you've cut are still there.
When there's plenty of space in your wardrobe
Yet your clothes are flung over a chair.
When you tell your wife that you love her
Then mutter girls names in your dreams
It's time to start packing your suitcase
For your number is up, so it seems.

A man is a creature of habits
All terribly bad I'm afraid,
Who never quite knows how to put in effect
All the good resolutions he's made.
A wife is a saint and an angel
But even an angel can fall
And its no good expecting her favours
When you've driven her right up the wall!

~~~~~~~~~~~~~~~~~

THERE WAS A TIME

Let us grieve for values lost, for verities destroyed,
For trust and honour maimed and scarred, for truth we now avoid.
Let us bury feelings slain, with innocence debased,
And all the glorious family pride, this awful age disgraced.

There was a time when people cared, and helped the sick and weak,
When children safely walked the streets, and homes were never bleak.
When lonely souls were visited, and made to feel worthwhile,
And cutting words weren't left to rust, but polished with a smile.

Drop by drop there drained away the sweet filled well of joy,
That once refreshed the thirsty soul when I was yet a boy.
Somewhere along the fleeting years the gold was changed to grey,
As people turned their heads aside, and looked the other way.

Now swearing is a part of life where once sweet words were spoke,
And as we listen horrified, there's filth in every joke.
Television screens portray the seamier side of life,
Until you feel ashamed to watch, with children or with wife.

I remember better days, when chapel was our rock,
When we walked tall with Christ our Lord, and no-one thought to mock.
When ten commandments were our guide, along a twisting road,
And we knelt down before that throne, from whence our loving flowed.

So let us pray this love returns, that folk will once more care,
So countless children, yet unborn, will find a faith to share.
Where they can lay foundations down and help to build a dream,
Where values lost are all restored, and kindness reigns supreme!

~~~~~~~~~~~~~~~~~

UNBIDDEN TO THE FEAST

Where the hopfield kissed the meadow,
Fountain leapt the icy spring,
From the massive oak tree's shadow,
Where the buzz-saw horseflies wing.
    Here we filled our Woolworth kettles,
    Or the cheap enamel pots,
    Tender knees on stinging nettles,
    Sprouting hosts of angry spots.

Here the acorns in their pipe bowls,
Squirrel dropped for winters' dream,
Like the mystery that life holds,
Floated downward in the stream.
    While the mist of flesh roused midges,
    With their bloodlust unappeased,
    Drank their fill as swelling ridges,
    Rose unbidden to the feast.

Here were passed the spicy rumours
In the sing song chant of Wales,
As with flash of navy bloomers,
Women knelt to fill their pails.
    All the scandalous sensation
    As we stood in shocked amaze.
    Character assassination,
    Interspersed with damning praise.

Watch fobbed waistcoats sprouted striped sleeves
From their vest sprung flannel shirts,
Seat shone trousers sat on dried leaves,
Or the horse manured dirt.
    From stained teeth cheap fags protruded,
    Lighting up each blue scarred face,
    And where Woodbine smoke intruded,
    Dust pocked lungs absorbed each trace.

Where the hopfield mated meadow
Leapt the sap in tired bones,
Fugitives from valley shadow,
Drawing water from the stones.
    Filling life's old Woolworth kettles,
    Cheapjack pots and battered pails,
    Prayerlike postured in the nettles,
    Kneel the dispossessed of Wales.

~~~~~~~~~~~~~~~~~

TO MY PEERS

Let us be honest with ourselves,
Old age has come to stay,
And there is nothing we can do
To make it go away.
And yet, and yet, one springtime morn,
When sunlight follows rain,
The little children that we were,
Are somehow born again.

We see the world through different eyes
As we our souls refresh,
And everyone of us is free
Not prisoners of the flesh.
Our spirits course through leafy glades,
Our thoughts climb childhood's hill,
As we run barefoot to the past
Through fields of daffodils.

Perhaps we look at photographs
From sometime in our teens,
Bright images of how we looked,
Well travelled time machines;
Or lift the lid of some old box
That's now a treasure chest,
To see within its musty depths
A faded wedding dress.

There is no going back through time,
Except within our dreams,
But springtime flowers, golden dawns,
Still quicken blood it seems.
And sometimes on a ballroom floor
Life still holds many charms,
As you go dancing through the night,
Your partner in your arms.

Yet if we're honest with ourselves,
We'll not deny this truth,
That we are not the same today
As once we were in youth.
And yet, and yet, all this can change
When sweet upon the breeze
Nostalgic scents of yesteryear
Recharge the air we breathe.

~~~~~~~~~~~~~~~~~

TAKE ME BACK

O! take me back to Merthyr, where still my spirit dreams,
Below the wimberry mountains, beside the singing streams.
Bear my feelings homeward on breezes that were fresh
When I was but a valley child and bathed in tenderness.

O! take me up to Dowlais, through streets I loved so well,
In tramcars that would turn around outside the Bush Hotel.
Place me with my comrades where processions would begin,
That I might sound a marching roll on my small drum of tin.

O! fly me to Penydarren, on wings of joy and love,
The Morlais Brook to cleanse my soul, the green, green grass above.
The County School perched on its hill, the well worn steps that climbed
To where I dreamed long hours away and left my youth behind.

Take me to Pontsarn again, to where seven arches rise,
To cast gigantic shadows through the vale where beauty lies.
Let me feel in retrospect the steam upon my face
From trains that bore me lovingly to that enchanted place.

Take me back to Darren View, the street where I was born,
To where my parents cherished me with hearts forever warm.
Let me see my brothers and all my sisters too,
The way they were when they were young and life was good and true.

O! bear me on forever, through valleys that were green,
On those beloved cream, brown trains, back in the age of steam.
And let me travel homewards beyond the curve of time
That I might meet the boy I was before life lost its shine!

~~~~~~~~~~~~~~~~

MY SON

My son was a pleasure to be with,
So loving and gentle was he.
A gift sent from God, in whose footsteps he trod,
As he lived with his mother and me.
He never once caused any trouble,
His honour was precious to him
And the mirror to truth, that he was in his youth,
Reflected the glory within.

His progress at school was amazing,
He always came top of his class.
Yet still found the time to write music sublime
No matter what subjects he passed.
His mind was a perfect computer
That filled every cell in his brain
With programs so vast, the knowledge amassed
Could be used again and again.

In his teens he was born of the spirit
And claimed by the Lord who is Life.
For his soul was redeemed by the precious red streams
That flowed from the body of Christ.
He has lived to become a professor,
Esteemed, with a book to his name,
But the blessing he is, and the joy that he gives
Means more to us now than his fame.

My son is a pleasure to visit
The family he has, makes us proud
For they follow on, where his footsteps have gone
The furrow his loving has ploughed.
We know we are blessed by his spirit
The essence of goodness and trust
For both of us feel as we prayfully kneel
He is there with his Saviour and us!

~~~~~~~~~~~~~~~~~

MOTHER'S DAY

We walk with a heart filled with love,
Through the mist of a million hours,
Rememb'ring the times we have shared,
And the joy that we know to be ours.

Birthdays have vanished like snowflakes,
That melt with the heat of the years,
Flashing like stars past the windows,
That run with the flow of our tears.

We gaze through the glass that is memory,
To see past the gate of the soul,
Where those we have loved walk forever,
With friends who will never grow old.

The run of God's world is unending,
The circle of time binds us all,
With the sweet cup of life overflowing,
With memories that we recall.

The streets that we knew are immortal,
The houses we lived in still there.
The flames that are love warm the bright rooms,
Long fanned by the pleasures we share.

The old ones still sit in their corners,
For we are a part of them yet,
The words that they spoke are remembered,
Through days that are hard to forget.

And you are the clasp of the chain, Mam,
That holds every link in its place.
The gold that is love ever shining,
The passage of time can't erase.

We stand where your dear hand can touch us,
To know as your great day comes round,
That the truth of the joy that we're seeking
Can there in your warm heart be found.

~~~~~~~~~~~~~~~~~~~~~~~~

GABRIEL SATAN

My dog was a saint and an angel
Though he could be awkward as well.
When good he was fashioned in heaven,
When bad he was straight out of hell.
A cat was a creature he hated,
A child was the font of his love,
So we called him both Gabriel and Satan,
For these names seemed to fit like a glove.

The tricks he could do were amazing,
No circus trained act could do more.
Back somersaults over a table,
Or jumping to open a door.
He would run to fetch my newspaper
From the mat on the floor of the hall,
With never a tear of its pages,
Or damaged for reading at all.

It's true he would bite every postman,
For uniformed men were his bane.
While the seats of their baggy serge trousers
Were savaged again and again.
Yet infants could ride on his haunches,
Then tug with great force at his ears,
And he would put up with their teasing,
Though his eyes were heavy with tears.

His end, when it came, showed his mettle.
When our son rolled into a stream,
And Gabriel Satan who loved him,
Was roused by the sound of his screams;
And jumped without thought to his rescue
Where the current was flowing so fast,
Then clung with his paws to our baby,
To bring him out safely at last.

But he gave up his soul in that river,
For just as we caught up our child,
The dog was dragged down by the current,
For the waters were running so wild.
And when we recovered his body,
Then placed him with love in his grave,
The name on the cross wasn't Satan,
But simply read "Gabriel the brave".

My dog was a saint and an angel
No tribute is greater than this.
When bad he was straight out of Hades,
When good he was fashioned from bliss.
We parents will love him forever,
He stayed true to us to the end.
And we know he is with his Creator,
For he gave up his life for a friend!

~~~~~~~~~~~~~~~~~~~~~~~

THE PRICE OF FAITH

As you plough a lonely furrow through the winter of your life,
Without a caring husband or without a loving wife,
Remember there is Someone with a glorious life to share
Who only asks the price of faith if you have this to spare.

There is no void He cannot fill, no soul that He can't reach,
Though there be millions needing Him, He still has time for each.
Believe in Him and you will see Him step down from the cross
That He might take upon Himself, the burden of your loss.

No need to face the world alone, no need to fear the end,
When Christ is walking at your side, you need no other friend.
There is no grief He cannot bear, no doubt He can't dispel,
And He will save His people from the very jaws of hell.

Though doors may close and shut you in as age replaces youth,
The gates of Heaven open up so you might glimpse the truth,
That this life's but a pilgrimage to that abiding place
Where we will take from nail scarred hands, God's perfect gift of grace.

The hours of darkness can be lit, the heart with warmth instilled.
Just read the pages of the Book and you will be fulfilled.
A voice is clamouring to be heard, a hand in love extends
To draw you gently into Heaven when this life's journey ends.

So faithful friends, feel not alone, the fellowship of Christ
Is one great circle round the world that binds and holds you tight.
Each living cell within the chain dovetails into the whole,
The flesh of faith, the bones of truth, and one immortal soul.

Don't plough a lonely furrow through the winter of your days,
Without a loving Saviour or without a hymn of praise.
Remember He is waiting with eternal life to share
And only asks the price of faith, if you have this to spare.

~~~~

STRANGE THINGS

In the land of Pooh, all the menfolk do
Strange things in the dead of the night.
They crawl up the trees on their hands and knees,
And put the monkeys to flight.
Then just for a lark, they strip off the bark
And chew it all into a pulp.
Then offer a share to the great Pooh bear
Who lives in the hollow trunk.

In the huts below all the women know
Why the men perform this rite.
As they sit and stare while the great Pooh bear
Just swallows this mess outright.
As the beast gulps deep and settles to sleep,
The men in the tree shout "Boo!"
And the bear drops dead, like a ton of lead
In the dark of the land of Pooh.

In the hollow trunk, the men get drunk
On the juice of the beery bee,
And hang on their chests, all the kookabar nests
Festooning the Ratabang tree.
Then fall to the ground with a sickening sound,
To the wail of their wives lament.
And are buried there with the great Pooh bear,
On the spot of their last descent.

And the moral is, it's not a good whizz
To shin up a Ratabang tree.
Or offer to share with a bristly bear,
The juice of the beery bee.
For Kookabar nests will fall off your chests
And someone will surely shout "Boo!"
As you drop stone dead on your broken head
In the terrible land of Pooh!

~~~~~~~~~~~~~~~~

WHEN ALL ELSE FAILS

I've seen Cyfarthfa Castle from a slagheap's grimy ridge,
Walked from Pontsarn's arches down the vale to Cefn bridge,
Stood in Vaynor's churchyard with companions of my youth,
Prayed in Penyard chapel to the God of light and truth.

I've felt my father write through me the words that now you see,
Walked with him the wimberry hills, again in memory;
Warmed my thoughts on loving fires that burned within his soul,
Longed to give him back the health that age and sickness stole.

I've played in Dowlais steel mills where the girders rusted red,
Roamed Cyfarthfa's ironworks with ghosts of men long dead;
Stood in mildewed changing rooms where collier voices rang,
Climbed through slimy, broken walls where pit lamps used to hang.

I've been on chapel outings since the days when I was small,
Building castles on the beach in Barry and Porthcawl.
There have been times I've wondered as I roamed this troubled land.
If these were castles in the air, or built on shifting sand.

I've lived with my grandparents in their home above the hill,
Sharing love together as a family always will.
I ran their errands willingly, they never asked for much,
And smiles that then rewarded me, were lodestones that I touched.

I've seen my mother washing clothes in our old splintered tub,
Hands that gripped a scrubbing board, with Sunlight soap to rub,
Foaming suds like mountain snow on arms the years chafed red,
Whilst acids burned within her bones and dreams drowned in her head.

I've kept in step with jazzbands as through Merthyr town they wound,
Watched their competitions on Cyfarthfa's football ground.
Seen my uncle Hopkin twirl his baton without pause,
As he led the great procession with his Spanish picadors.

I've heard the sad, sweet, throbbing of mouthorgans blowing wild
Down the dark, old terraced streets into each listening child,
Striking chords in youthful hearts, for music cleans the soul
In valleys where the streams run black and hills are made of coal.

I've served in Merthyr's Fire Brigade, with men of steel and grit,
Went to fires from Dowlais Top, right down to Perrots Pitch.
Learned the skills that served me well through years as yet unborn,
And still remember stalwart men who made my life so warm.

I've lingered in the Market Hall when I had cash to spend,
Making every penny count, as pleasure knew no end.
I sat to peas and faggots in odiferous little stalls,
And ate my way to paradise within their whitewashed walls.

I've listened to men singing (and the melody was sweet),
As they came off collier buses at the corner of our street,
Offering up a hymn of praise that they could breathe the air
That blew off ancient Cambrian hills that once were green and fair.

I've slept with my two brothers in a brass-framed lumpy bed,
Walked with my dear sisters where my childhood memories fled;
Studied in the Queens Road School when I was only three,
O! how these sweet remembrances come flooding back to me.

I've played those games that please the young, on dusty roads and tips,
Skipping with frayed orange rope and cracking tops with whips;
Jumping over hopscotch squares as girls sang plaintive rhymes,
Perhaps their voices echo still, down corridors of time.

I've suffered strokes from stinging canes when I have played the fool
In playground, hall and classroom of the Borough's County School.
Many times played truant when the days were warm and long,
And never thought to question if the things I did were wrong.

I've ridden bikes with threadbare tyres down rutted valley roads,
From Dowlais to Treharris past the landscape I adored;
Cycling on forever through the empire of the sun,
Freewheeling down the hills of joy on wheels that sweetly spun.

I've hungered for elusive things like peace and happiness,
Chased the butterfly of time through fields of tenderness;
Sought the nightingale of life, yet heard the cuckoo's call,
Ate apples from forbidden trees and shared poor Adam's fall.

I've never tried to find redress for all that's owed to me,
I've known the greatest love of all, and this was given free.
People cared when times were hard, to this I'll always cling,
That kindness ruled the humblest heart, when poverty was king.

I've never tried to lose my roots, my accent I've retained,
And Merthyr town is not forgot, for Welsh I have remained.
I've left my country in the flesh, and yet when all else fails,
I'll look inside my childhood dreams, and find I'm home in Wales!

~~~~~~~~~~~~~~~~

HARD TO RESIST

My wife simply loves to solve crosswords,
She is doing one now as I write.
Spectacles perched on the tip of her nose,
As she struggles to get the words right.
The clues are much harder than usual,
The lines on her forehead run deep,
And the pen in her hand isn't moving,
Perhaps she has fallen asleep!

But no, I can see there's some movement,
The pen is now down on the page.
My wife wears an air of great triumph,
And looks like a quizzical sage.
Two across has been conquered in seconds,
Three down is the next one to go,
And she looks so divine at this moment,
No wonder that I love her so.

The rest of the puzzle is easy,
She has broken the back of it now.
The pen moves so fast I can't see it,
The lines are removed from her brow.
Her breathing is slower, more measured,
There's a smile of delight on her lips.
Perhaps I'll go over and kiss her,
I find her so hard to resist!

She is down to the very last question,
This clue has been harder than most.
I'm hoping she'll ask me to solve it,
But she never gives up the ghost.
It is done! she is sitting bolt upright,
And looking quite gorgeous to me.
How lucky I am to be married
To someone as brilliant as she!

~~~~~~~~~~~~~~~~~

ONE OF US
Tribute to Princess Diana

Forget the glitz and the razzmatazz,
The awesome power that a Princess has.
Remember instead the core of gold
That burned so bright within her soul.

Think of the people she used to touch,
The sick and the weak she loved so much.
Forget the clamour, the glamour, the glitz
She lived in us all as well as the Ritz.

Queen of our hearts, a peoples' Princess,
Each word that she spoke was like a caress.
Ignore all the glitz and the razzmatazz,
Others have these and such things pass.

The flowers will die that we lay at her gate,
Their petals will fall as surely as fate.
In the Spring of each year, in the green of the grass,
We'll remember her joy, not the razzmatazz.

So rest in peace, Diana the brave,
Warm in our prayers, not cold in the grave.
You bypassed the clamour, the glamour, the glitz,
And made us all feel we lived at the Ritz.

Nothing and no-one can equal your fame,
We look at the stars and remember your name.
Not for the razzmatazz or the fuss
But simply because you were one of us!

~~~~~~~~~~~~~~~~

LAST WHISTLE

I little thought when I was small,
And sometimes played the fool.
That I would one day be a dad,
And meet my kids from school.
For I was never met myself,
There was no need to be,
The world was that much safer then
And no-one troubled me.

There were no crowded city streets,
No cars to run me down.
I lived upon a mountain then,
Not down in Merthyr Town.
There were no evil men to fear,
At least none that I knew,
And I was safe to walk back home
When school's last whistle blew.

The folk I met upon the road
Would stop and talk to me.
Sometimes to pass on sound advice,
Or ask me home to tea.
For we were not scared children then,
Who feared to be abused
And offers made in such good faith
Were never yet refused.

Now I'm a grandad for my pains,
And I am proud to say,
That my grandchildren all trust me
Indoors or out at play.
Perhaps they see the child in me,
That trusting little boy
Who walked in safety through his youth
Into the realms of joy!

~~~~~~~~~~~~~~~~

THE TOE OF SOMEONE'S BOOT

Indifferent to scolding tongues, my butty Joe and me
Would monkey-like climb over walls where'er we chanced to be,
To take from gardens veg. and flowers with just a little fruit,
Or if we were too slow to run, the toe of someone's boot.

My butty Joe was only five whilst I was almost six,
But in our minds we thought as men and practised mannish tricks.
We rolled brown paper cigarettes from herbs as foul as sin,
To vomit violently each time we puffed the black smoke in.

We bathed in many mountain streams to cleanse our skins of mud,
We fought each others battles and we staunched each others blood.
We made dark tents of hessian cloth that shook in every breeze,
And shivered bravely through long nights when dew on grass would freeze.

Our parents never tried to cut the knot that bound us tight,
But marvelled at our happiness as childish dreams took flight.
Joe was my heart and I his soul and spirit did we share,
That burned unquenched in both of us as time brought grief to spare.

Form Woolworth's garish counter tops we took the goods displayed,
Secreting gleaming magic toys for which we never paid,
Plastic whistles, clockwork cars and many a tin gazoot,
And in some hide-out in the park would bury all our loot.

Perhaps these toys are still unfound though fifty years have sped;
And maybe Joe who fell in war still guards them now he's dead.
The yellow gorse that covers all grows thicker with the years,
The soil around its roots enriched by my rememb'ring tears.

Indifferent now to curious eyes, I go to France each spring,
To place upon Joe's lonely grave the flowers and fruit I'd bring,
With plastic whistle, clockwork car, a shining tin gazoot,
And as he was too brave to run, the toe of someone's boot!

~~~~~~~~~~~~~~~~~

PORK AND BEANS

I wasn't created for dancing
Or rhythm would flow through my genes.
My feet would be kind to each other,
Like pork is at peace with baked beans.
I really don't know how it happened,
My brothers and sisters can dance,
Perhaps I am simply a mutant
That nature created by chance!

I've tried more than once to correct this
By watching the ballet for months.
Spun like a top on the tips of my toes
And fractured both insteps at once.
My knees are both hams in sheep's clothing,
My ankles have swollen so much
They look like balloons filled with putty,
So tender and sore to the touch.

My wife is alarmed by my bruises
For they are so black and so blue,
I exhibit them now in a freak show,
And am billed as 'The Human Tattoo'.
She has bought me the very best ointment,
And rubbed it deep into the skin,
But this only damaged the tissues,
And altered the shape of my chin!

We went to a sequence dance evening,
(The people there should have been warned!)
We tore through their ranks like a battering ram,
So violent the steps we performed.
Our leaders were carried off lifeless,
And though they were later revived,
They've had to give up sequence dancing,
And do something else with their lives!

In time we both learned to stay upright,
The crutches I had helped a lot.
I used them to trip other couples,
Whilst dancing a waltz or gavotte.
Of course, being awkward and clumsy,
I mow people down like before,
But at least there are now paramedics
To scrape their remains off the floor!

A terrible thing once befell me
Whilst doing the twist in a hall.
My braces got tangled so badly,
I had the most desperate fall.
My elbows got stuck in my armpits,
My feet were impaled in my groin,
And such was the force of the impact,
There wasn't the sign of a join.

I am told that my larger intestine,
Is lovingly coiled around my spleen.
My liver and lungs have changed places,
Both kidneys are hanging between.
Two fingers are stuck up each nostril,
There's a thumb and a toe in each ear,
And before I can go to the toilet,
My front must be freed from my rear.

I would not advise clumsy people
To learn sequence dancing like me.
It's better to dabble in parachute drops,
Or wrestle with sharks in the sea.
Though visitors come to my sick bed,
And bring me both flowers and fruit,
I'd rather they got me untwisted,
So I could get into my suit.

Dancing involves perfect timing,
A skill I have never possessed.
My brain can't connect with my tootsies,
Its message gets stuck in my chest.
Stewed apples are brilliant with custard,
Mint sauce is delicious with lamb,
But rhythm and me are still strangers,
How twisted and bitter I am!

~~~~~~~~~~~~~~~~~~~~~~

THE SERMON ON THE MOUNT

Matthew Chapter 5 Vs. 1-11

The poor in spirit I will bless by opening the gate
That leads into that heavenly realm where God is always great.
Then I will give them all I have and as their spirits soar
Through my shed blood they'll be reborn to live for evermore.

When those you love have passed away and this world falls apart,
I'll swiftly come with healing hands to mend the broken heart.
To comfort those who sadly mourn with words of my belief,
That I might take upon myself the burden of their grief.

Blessed are the lowly meek for they will own the Earth,
Though they may now abase themselves it's I who'll judge their worth.
The arrogant I'll sweep away, but those who bend the knee
Will tap the source of heavenly power that flows through God to me.

Those who hunger and who thirst for righteousness and truth,
Will eat and drink in paradise of God's immortal fruit;
And by its richness will be filled until the hungry soul
Will never seek its sustenance from dark temptation's bowl.

Blessed are the merciful, their names by God are known,
And He'll remember them in Heaven where they'll have mercy shown.
He gives to each what they deserve and asks no more than this
That man behaves with love to man, for those who love are His.

The pure in heart will see their God for they are blest by sight
That only comes when evil goes and souls are bathed in light.
For as they put their trust in me and I my faith in them
Then I am sent once more to Earth and born in Bethlehem.

Blest are they who banish strife for they will bear the name
Of Sons of God and heirs of heaven, for this is theirs to claim;
And I will be their own High Priest whose tongue will never cease
To intercede with God for them, for He is Lord of Peace.

I give my kingdom to the brave who leap to my defence,
And suffer much for righteousness, for them I'll recompense.
Their trials will be shared by me, they will not cry in vain
For I will come on wings of grace to lift them out of pain.

You've borne the insults of the mob, you've turned the other cheek,
Because you've gone through hell for me these words of cheer I speak.
Rejoice and be exceeding glad for as you love the Lord
Then you will stand before the throne, for Heaven is your reward!

~~~~~~~~~~~~~~~~

WHEN I WAS YOUNG

When I was young, dreams in my head
Spun round a magic coil.
Where innocence the bearings fed
With youth's immortal oil.
The grass it was a special green
With blades like silken hair,
And where the rivers tumbled clean,
Each murmur seemed a prayer.

When I was young the world was old
And lay a spell on me,
That changed base metal into gold
And set my spirit free.
So I could paint a naked nerve,
Embrace a baby's smile.
Slide down a rainbows graceful curve,
Or build a desert isle.

When I was young and full of hope
My mother's touch was soft.
With gentle hands perfumed with soap
She held my soul aloft.
My father was a craggy hill
Wreathed in a Woodbine's smoke.
And on his strength and on his will
The darkest stormclouds broke.

When I was young each wounding word
Drew blood out of the heart.
While in that place where feelings stirred
I felt the teardrops start.
Who knows what dreams are murdered here?
Who sees emotion slain?
Who lines that road to mock and jeer
Where walks a child to pain?

When I was young I polished stars
And flew the crescent moon.
Rode rocketships through space to Mars,
Sent aliens to their doom.
I read the lurid magazines
Where fantasy was king.
Chased Hellish creatures through my dreams
And scorched a dragons wing.

When I was young the friends I made
Would give their lives for me;
And I for them for as we played
We grew a greenlife tree.
Its roots were nourished by our sweat,
Its stem fed by our blood,
And where the leaves and branches met,
Life's blossom came to bud.

When I was young the world was not
But this I failed to see;
And though it hasn't changed a lot
It's killed the child in me.
I see the hills I used to climb,
I mourn for all that's lost,
And span again the gulf of time,
Where I to manhood crossed!

~~~~~~~~~~~~~~~~~~~~~~~

BELOVED COMPANION

A three piece suite is expendable
For none seem to last very long.
The settees will sag in the middle,
The springs in their bases aren't strong
The fabric will fade in the sunshine
That comes through your windows at noon,
While the intricate patterns created
Resemble the face of the moon.

The armchairs that seemed built for comfort,
The day that you bought them brand new,
Now seem to develop hard ridges
That bring out great bruises on you.
Their piping has run out of stitches,
Their valances short by a mile,
While the arms are so ugly and awkward
They seem to have gone out of style.

Children will stand on their cushions
Then jump up and down in the air.
The stuffing comes out at the edges
Like straw from an old teddybear.
The covers show stains quite revolting
From sticky young fingers and such,
For infants just can't abide washing
And soil everything that they touch.

And yet you are loath now to change it
For it has become an old friend.
A battered companion, homely and warm
That's ready to serve to the end.
So you think of the comfort it's given
To you and the love of your life
And swear you will keep it through sickness and health
Just as you did with your wife

~~~~~~~~~~~~~~~

MY MAFIA AUNT

I know it seems beyond belief
That my Aunt Bron was Mafia chief
Of all South Wales from Brecon down
To Cardiff and to Swansea Town.

She organised the ice-cream men,
The Eye-tie caffs and gambling dens,
The Chapel Sisterhoods and such,
Though Bands of Hope she wouldn't touch.

She raided rival betting shops,
Collected bribes, paid off the Cops.
Highjacked lorries, trains and planes
And stashed away illicit gains.

She tampered with the Royal Mail's
And sold the gold mines of North Wales
To tourists and to simple folk
Who never could quite see the joke.

No rival mobster could deter
The onward march of such as her,
But fled with money, stocks and shares
To Rio or to Buenos Aires.

She'd learned in countless rugby scrums
The wicked art of digging thumbs
Into the private parts of those
Who interfered with her clothes.

She did by learning martial arts
Do damage to men's tenderest parts
And when their cries of anguish rose
She calmly punched them on the nose.

When fighting in a boxing booth
She never held herself aloof
But used her height of four foot nine
To hit below the plimsoll line.

She'd take advantage of her sex
By rabbit punching backs of necks
And digging thumbs in belly B's
Whilst making eyes at referees.

No doubt she had to be on guard
Because her life had been so hard,
But did she have to use her head
To knock them out? opponents said.

Well all this rough and tumble strife,
Now fitted her for Mafia life;
And thugs who'd make a meal of me,
Were proud to work for such as she.

She thrived and blossomed like a rose,
Put on two stone and bought new clothes.
Used all her weight to batter down
The barricaded doors in town.

he never used a Tommy-gun,
The old one, two, was much more fun
And in a trice she'd have her way
With those who had refused to pay.

With hands around reluctant throats,
Her bags would fill with ten pound notes,
And as she squeezed she'd shed a tear
For those she ruled by force or fear.

She knew quite well it couldn't last,
That all the empires of the past
Had reached a peak then fell to dust,
As all top heavy structures must.

So on a moonless, misty night
She packed her bags, prepared for flight,
And warmly clad in six thick frocks
She made her way to Barry Docks.

From there a motor cruiser took
My Mafia Aunt to Hollands Hook.
Where with the fortune she was worth,
She disappeared off this earth.

Now grieves South Wales for it has found
Without my wicked Aunt around,
It's deadly dull and they all yearn,
For thrill packed days with her return!

~~~~~~~~~~~~~~~~~~~~~~~

LORD OF THE DANCE

If paper was made for wrapping,
With stars on backgrounds of gold,
I would make a wondrous parcel,
Of an art that's centuries old.
I would take it to lofty cathedrals,
Where angelic hosts standing by,
Would fly with my gift through the reaches
Of God's indestructible sky.

Happy people would collect it,
Armed with drums and saxophones.
They would take it to a ballroom,
That the King of glory owns.
He would then unwrap the parcel,
Cutting through its silver strings,
Taking out the art of dancing,
Flown to Him on angel wings.

Trumpets would join in the music,
Led by Gabriel on his horn.
Saints would trip the light fantastic,
Sequence dances would be born.
Waltzes, foxtrots, saunters, rumbas,
Quicksteps, swings, cha chas and blues,
Mambos, tangoes, jives and sambas,
Dance performed by twinkling shoes.

Soon the folk in every country
Lifted up on clouds of joy,
Every wife and every husband,
Every girl and every boy,
Would be gripped by dancing fever,
As strict tempo music played.
Every couple, all their leaders,
In an endless dance parade.

I believe we're lucky people
To receive this gift of gold.
Shared in something very precious,
Touched a cord within the soul.
Made new friends in old surroundings,
Gave them love that they returned.
May the art of sequence dancing
Be the finest we have learned.

We are blest by hands that take us
Through some great, celestial door.
Where the Lord of every dancer,
Comes to lead us round the floor.
Let us now embrace our partners,
With a warmth that flows from Him,
Through each golden dawn and sunset,
'Til the lamps of Heaven dim!

~~~~~~~~~~~~~~~~~~~~~~~

AGE CAN STILL BE FUN

You know you're growing older when you can't stand on a chair,
Or even climb a ladder more than three foot in the air.
The stairs and hills seem steeper, your knees just won't obey,
And next year's hip replacement is still twelve months away.

Your hair comes out in handfuls, your teeth have long since strayed,
Your memory has got so bad you can't find your hearing aid.
There's dry rot in your spinal cord, and death watch beetle too,
For when you run to catch a bus, your legs and toes turn blue.

You're ready now for meals on wheels, and maybe some home help,
For though you try to carry on, you just can't help yourself.
By now you're past your sell by date, your shelf life has expired,
Why didn't someone tell you this, the date that you retired.

Of course there's compensations, day centres run for you,
Volunteers to drive you there, and willing carers too.
People who will entertain, to make your life worthwhile,
For even age is bearable, if polished by a smile.

There's more time now for hobbies, if you're still fit that is,
Though gardening becomes a chore, now that you've lost your fizz.
Yet there are chairs to sit on, grandchildren call with gifts,
And you can still ascend the stairs on sturdy Stannah lifts.

Yet would you start your life again, to be a boy or girl?
I don't think somehow that you would, for 'twas a different world.
And after all you've found some peace, now that the struggling's done,
And there are many golden days, when age can still be fun!

~~~~~~~~~~~~~~~~~

THE LOVE SHE GAVE ME

The first that I knew of my mother,
Was the kiss of her lips on my face.
I knew it was she and no other,
By the feel, and the warmth and the taste.
Every day in her arms was a pleasure,
Her milk wasn't all she gave free;
And when it had dried up forever,
I gave her the love she gave me.

The debt that I owe to my mother,
Is a sum I can never repay.
But we'll go on loving each other
For Heaven's but a whisper away.
No rosebud could ever be fresher,
No blossom as lovely as she;
And when she was plucked by her Saviour,
I mourned for the love she gave me.

The best that I knew of my mother,
Was the feeling of joy that she gave.
I knew 'twas from her and no other,
For it comes to me now from the grave.
The smiles on her lips I still treasure,
Each one was the essence of she;
And in all my prayers I endeavour
To give her the love she gave me.

The last that I knew of my mother,
Was the chill in my heart as she died.
I knew it was she and no other,
Though the years had been cruel, not kind.
Yet pain which had come beyond measure
Could not hide her beauty from me;
And if we share Heaven together,
I'll give her the love she gave me!

~~~~~~~~~~~~~~~~~

I NEVER LEARNED

I never learned to rollerskate, the knack I haven't got,
I tried to use them several times and fell down quite a lot.
I cannot seem to balance well on all those tiny wheels,
Perhaps I would be better off with springs beneath my heels.

I've never learned to do the twist, for when such music plays,
I'm like a puppet on a string, whose joints face different ways.
And people turn and stare at me, so awkward is my stance,
Perhaps I would be better off if I gave up the dance.

I've never learned to draw or paint, I just don't have the touch.
The merest child surpasses me with crayons or a brush.
My wife paints toenails with more skill than I can paint a tree,
Perhaps I would be better off if I were her, not me.

I've never learned to drive a car, although I've sometimes tried.
The roads are safer without me, less people will have died.
I've had some lessons from the best and turned their hair quite white,
Perhaps I would be better off if I just rode a bike.

I've never learned the art of prayer, the words all come out wrong,
I've never learned a word or note of any popular song.
I've never learned to live and love, I've only learned to hate,
Perhaps I would be better off if I could rollerskate!

~~~~~~~~~~~~~~~~~

THE GHOST OF A GREAT WESTERN TRAIN

I long to go back on the Great Western track,
To the Merthyr I knew as a boy.
When engines were steam, and I lived in a dream,
Compounded of magic and joy.
Where valley towns lay by the permanent way,
With stations that bore friendly names;
And the Great Western staff in their liveried black,
Waved greetings to folk on the trains.

I ache to return where my memories burn,
On rails that are rusty and red.
Up gradients so steep, the train seems to creep,
And boilers with coal must be fed.

Passed cottages thatched, to a beauty unmatched
In the heart of a peaceful Pontsarn,
Where once we would meet, for our Sunday School treat,
In the shade of a weathered old barn.

I want to re-book all the journeys I took,
To Barry, Porthcawl, and Penarth.
Where trains thundered down, through village and town,
By the banks of the babbling Taff.
And slagheaps arose, where the wimberry grows,
On hills that were magic to me,
While the train slowed its pace, with ineffable grace,
As we came to the welcoming sea.

I must re-embark, as the evening grows dark,
From platforms where coaches await;
And carriage springs groan, as whistles are blown,
To warn all the folk who are late.
Fine sand trickles through, from my socks to each shoe,
While skin that is burned starts to hurt;
And tears that are shed, for the joys that have fled,
Are dried on the sleeves of my shirt.

I'd sell half my soul for the smell of the coal,
As it flared in a furnace's core.
Providing the drive as the train comes alive
On wheels that are ready to go;
To take me back where, the people all care,
And childhood's remembered again.
A journey through time, to that Merthyr of mine,
On the Ghost of a Great Western train.

~~~~~~~~~~~~~~~

UGLIER THAN A TREE

Important though he seems to be,
A man is uglier than a tree,
Much less alive than any bird,
Is more a creature of the herd.

A man is vainer than a girl,
Yet somewhat duller than a pearl.
Is much more warlike than an ant,
Yet not so useful as a plant.

He breathes more oxygen than most,
The when he dies is still a ghost.
Now you would think he'd have more sense
Than stay to haunt the present tense.

Man still pollutes the atmosphere,
Then chains whole nations to his fear,
Seeks out new ways to kill his kind,
And breaks all laws that God designed.

So many insects of the earth,
In headlong rush to death from birth,
Can yet conform to Nature's plan,
In such a way as shames a man.

A mayfly's crowded day of life
Is frenzied, yes, but free from strife.
Could we but boast a part of this,
Then God would come, and we'd be His.

A man is said to have a soul,
If that be true, then this he stole;
For man has robbed since Adam's time,
And fattened long on every crime.

A child was born at Bethlehem,
That hopes might grow from this straight stem.
Instead, man nailed two planks of wood,
And crucified the wondrous good.

Perhaps the blood from such sweet flesh,
Will one day wash with tenderness,
The dirty soul of grubby man,
As only blood from Heaven can.

Then man redeemed by God's own Son,
Will see that his true will be done,
And build a world that's free from pain,
That Christ might walk this earth again.

~~~~~~~~~~~~~~~~~

SAMMY THE SNAKE

Sammy the snake is an adder
And yet is a dunce with his sums.
He's hopeless at multiplication,
It's something to do with his gums.
When anyone mentions division,
He splits into two like a shot,
While the decimal point that he carries
Is more of a dash than a dot!

Snakes shouldn't meddle with science,
Their brains are like mouldy old cheese.
I think they'd do better at English,
(They reel and they writhe with great ease.)
They bite like a streak of greased lightening,
With poisonous thoughts in their brains,
Then strike without ceasing their labour,
And never much care who complains.

They were cursed in the garden of Eden
For bringing about Adam's fall,
But they never bother about it,
It's something no snake can recall.
They shed their old skins in a second,
Then leave them behind in the dust,
And wriggle with joyous abandon,
As adders, refurbished, all must.

A snake is a coldblooded reptile,
And Sammy's no different to most.
Through he has good points I could mention,
He never eats hamsters on toast.
One day the good Lord will forgive him,
By gifting him legs and two feet,
So he can walk tall out of Eden,
And sit down at table to eat!

~~~~~~~~~~~~~~~~

MY CANDLE IN THE DARK
To my wife at Christmas

Who is the centre of my life? My heart believes it's you,
For you are all in all to me, in everything I do.
No other woman fills my eye, no other woman will,
For I have loved you from the start, and dear, I love you still.

The slightest pressure of your hand, a glance from your blue eyes,
Are still enough to stir my soul with joy that never dies.
Your lips brush mine, and I am drowned in some great thrilling sea,
And I will lie in those sweet depths because you're part of me.

I'll always bless the day you came to share this life of mine.
You've painted time with gold for me, and made each day divine.
I see you as you always are, an incandescent spark,
For you are lovely in my sight, my candle in the dark.

You've given me life's richest prize, the children I adore.
Two splendid images of you, no man could ask for more.
I see you in their tenderness, I hear them in your voice,
And as they think and act like you, they make my heart rejoice.

This Christmas I am still your boy, and you're my darling girl,
Nothing changes what I feel, your arms remain my world.
A wondrous gift is what you are, you make my spirit sing,
And I will wrap you in my life and tie with joy the string.

The bond between us stronger grows, we are the living proof
That love can blossom like a rose, from roots put down in youth.
And as each night gives way to dawn, then this my prayer will be,
That I will stay enshrined in you, and you enthroned in me!

~~~~~~~~~~~~~~~~~

A CHILD IN THE VALLEYS

When I was a child in the valleys
Through years when the rich knew us not,
Few birthdays were ever remembered
And poverty never forgot.
We never received any presents,
Excepting when Christmas came round,
And then 'twas a toy bought in Woolworths,
Or something our fathers had found.

Yet now they have parties in theme parks,
Then go to Macdonalds for food.
Every child has a gift to go home with,
And some are insufferably rude.
They have bicycles costing small fortunes,
Or hi-fi's with CDs and such,
With state of the art computers
That I'd be too frightened to touch.

They are driven to cinemas after,
In cars that are all power-steered,
Then given both popcorn and icecream,
Before the first film has appeared.
They guzzle their iced Coca Colas
And eat their hot dogs in a bun,
Then throw what remains on the carpet,
And think this is part of the fun.

Perhaps I am simply old fashioned
To think of the past with regret,
When everything given was valued,
And elders enjoyed some respect.
When nuts and some fruit in a stocking,
Or books from a secondhand store,
Meant more to us kids in the valleys
Than hi-fi's or cycles galore.

I think we're too good to our children
And kill them with kindness and love,
By giving them more than is needed,
When something, quite small, is enough.
Perhaps what they get comes too easy,
We really should practise restraint,
For some of their boorish behaviour,
Is testing the patience of saints.

And what of the children whose parents
Just cannot afford these treats?
Do they sit with rich friends in a classroom,
And wriggle with shame in their seats?
It's like keeping up with the Joneses,
With nothing financial to give,
And infants will dwell with this memory,
For all of the years that they live.

When I was a child in the valleys,
My friends were as poor as me.
But Oh! how we valued each other,
And gave of our loving most free.
It mattered but little that birthdays
By parents were sometimes forgot,
Every day that we shared was like Christmas,
What more has a millionaire got?

~~~~~~~~~~~~~~~~

IN THE MANSION OF OUR FATHER

In the quiet hush of evening as we contemplate the day,
Do we ever stop to wonder what went wrong along the way.
Do we search the inner conscience for the deeds we can't explain,
Would we do things any different if we could restart again?

In the aftermath of quarrels do we ask if we were wrong,
Do we put the blame on others or on us where it belongs.
Are we quick to show our anger, are we slow to make amends,
Do we take the hand that's offered, do we end the day as friends?

In a state of sheer euphoria as we look at all we have,
Do we think of hungry children who on this day will starve.
As we keep up with the Joneses and covet each new toy,
Will care for others cloud our thoughts as we our lives enjoy?

In the fullness of perfection as we view our every strength,
Are we saddened by the suff'ring of the lame and poor in health.
Are our eyes from pain averted, do we ever think that we
Could ease the burden of their lives and help to set them free?

In the comfort of the office, or on the factory floor,
Or maybe at the checkout in some supermarket store,
Do we feel the dole queues lengthen, do we know that we are blest
And does this make us ponder that we're luckier than the rest?

In the silence of the bedroom as before to sleep we go,
Do we ask for absolution from a God who loves us so.
Do we tell Him all that's happened, do we promise to atone,
Or do we beg for favours for our greedy selves alone?

In the mansions of our Father there are many rooms to spare,
Which for the great uncaring throng are castles in the air.
The world is indivisible, its people all are one,
Believing this, achieving this, we'll to the Father come!

~~~~~~~~~~~~~~~~

A WORLD I WILL NEVER FORGET

I won't let the door slam on my dad or my mam,
Or those musical evenings we shared,
Where joy was reclaimed as we all entertained,
For none would come unprepared.
I still see each face as if shining in grace
As we sang or recited in rhyme;
And proudly I say, that no concert today,
Could ever have been so sublime.

It really was jolly when my Aunty Molly
Played our piano at home,
While my Uncle Arthur, who came from Cyfarthfa
Sang songs in his rich baritone.
We gathered around them, as if to surround them
Though we were supporters, not players;
And felt we were kings, as we soared on faith's wings,
To harmonise voices with theirs.

Then Sylvy, my sister, with me to assist her,
Gave readings from God's holy word,
To thunder His praises in round rolling phrases,
Until all our pulses were stirred.
The verses rolled on, from Matthew to John,
As we followed the path Christ trod;
And we came to that place, where the faithful found grace,
In the arms of a welcoming God.

Sometimes it was Fanny, or my lovely granny,
Who lifted our spirits on high,
For granny's contralto, and Fanny's bel canto
Could charm the birds from the sky.
We chased every chorus, the pursuit was so glorious,
And as we caught up with them both,
'Twas angels ascending, and melody blending,
As those marvellous duettists burst forth.

Now I am much older, and people seem colder,
Than those wondrous days in the past,
When my dad and mother so loved one another,
We knew that our family would last.
And I will remember, for now and forever,
The feeling of joy as we met,
That comes to me still, from our home on the hill,
In a world I will never forget!

~~~~~~~~~~~~~~~~~~

IT MAKES YOU SICK

In darkest Africa you'll find
Most animals are quite unkind,
And have no manners when they chew
Such genteel folk like me and you.

They hold no napkins in their paws,
Don't even know what these are for
And even if these brutes could talk,
They'd never ask for knife or fork.

As tasty joint of man they eat,
They spit the gristle round their feet.
And when they drop fat toes or thumbs
They never sweep away the crumbs.

I've never seen a lion wash
Small spots of rain will make him cross.
He sulks away in den nearby,
And won't come out until it's dry!

A cheetah as its starts its run
The very thought of prayer will shun.
Though as it pounces on its prey,
Some mutter 'grace' or so they say.

No crocodile will clean its teeth,
And though this seems beyond belief,
Will run a mile just to avoid
A toothbrush bearing humanoid.

They've got no decency you see,
An elephant will strip a tree.
And when it's standing naked there
Goes charging off and leaves it bare.

When jackals dine in pack or group,
They never start a meal with soup,
But masticate some mangled twerp,
Without a 'pardon' if they burp.

You'd think they'd cook the folk they kill,
Not eat them raw as all beasts will,
Then garnish them with garlic sauce,
Just like the French when they eat horse.

It makes you sick to watch them feast,
Proud you're a man and not a beast,
And have a wife who on you waits
To clear your dirty cups and plates.

No! I'm disgusted with the lot,
I'm British see, not Hottentot.
It's time to act as leaders must
And make wild beasts behave like us!

~~~~~~~~~~~~~~~~~~~~

THE RUINED CITY FELL

Full long the city dreamed upon the shore,
Its ivory towers gleaming in the sun.
The sound of evening blended with the roar
Of crashing waves, each sounding like a gun.
Within its walls, well fed, at peace, content,
The festive people to their pleasures went.

Enchanting music, lyrically sung,
Strange instruments from earth's long distant past.
The older voices chanting with the young,
Exciting throbbing, hot blood running fast.
A thousand flashes shot towards the sun,
The carnival of life had just begun.

Gargoyles of painted hue paraded streets,
The trees within the park were decked with lights,
The peasants from the countryside shared seats,
And with the town's folk revelled in the sights.
From butts of mellow wood the wine ran free,
And drunken lovers rushed towards the sea.

Five thousand miles away, a madman stared
At one small button sunk within a wall,
And nuclear rockets, mission long prepared,
Lay in their launching cradles near the hall.
Red pennants hung from maps around the room,
Each flag a city, sliding to its doom.

The finger pressed and silver hurtled high,
A holocaust with madness as its source.
The rockets arched, and rained down from the sky,
The carnival of life had run its course;
And long before the sun had kissed the shore,
The ruined city fell, to rise no more.

~~~~~~~~~~~~~~~~

ABERFAN REMEMBERED

*Sung to a traditional Welsh air
"Watching the white wheat"*

We have lost the seeds of Man,
And grieved with all who loved them,
But in the heart of Aberfan,
We'll find new hope will blossom.

> *Chorus*
> *One day soon the grief may fade,*
> *As we dark shadows banish*
> *Then on that hill where loved ones played,*
> *The ghosts of time will vanish.*

I have prayed in that sad place
Where infant voices sounded;
And felt the sweet, amazing grace
With which they are surrounded.

> *Chorus*

There are other children now,
A whole new generation,
And these will surely show us how
We all can find salvation.

Thirty years have passed since then,
But memories are golden.
For we can still remember when
These tender souls were stolen.

> *Chorus*

Come you back to where we wait,
O! come you back tomorrow;
And we will meet at heaven's gate,
Where joy replaces sorrow!

~~~~~~~~~~~~~~~~

BLIND TOM

Blind Tom lived up in Colliers Row,
Blind Tom was proud and free,
Blind Tom had worked the pits below
The hill that sheltered me.
He didn't tap with painted staff,
He knew each stone and mound,
And safely walked the banks of Taff,
As he did underground.

His house was built of valley stone,
And roofed with quarry slate.
Within these walls he sat alone,
Before blackleaded grate.
He didn't brood on long past wrongs,
Or mourn his family dead,
But hummed the old Welsh choral songs
That sang inside his head.

Blind Tom had lived and dreamed his dreams,
Before his sight grew dim.
The singing stones of surging streams
Were violins to him.
The stab of water, sharp with ice,
Against age wrinkled skin,
Brought memories as sweet as spice,
And joys as old as sin.

The small blue scars of deep pit cuts,
Were tattooed on his brow,
The staring eyes that blindness shuts,
Saw not the coal fire's glow.
But voices murmured, people climbed
Up hillsides in his mind,
While down his cheeks, blue scarred, begrimed,
Flowed tears for all mankind.

Blind Tom lived in a world apart,
From those whose eyes could see,
But stamped like braille upon his heart
Were words for you and me.
'Beg not return for gifts that go,
Give thanks that you can feel
The warmth of sun, the kiss of snow,
The scars that time can heal.'

Blind Tom won't tap with painted rod
On doors that bar his way,
Won't ask reward of man or God
Or choose the easy way.
But he will give from his rich store,
Where love fills to the brim,
And turn no strangers from his door,
Who ask of alms from him.

Blind Tom lived up in Colliers Row,
Blind Tom was proud and free,
Blind Tom cut coal from pits below
The hill that sheltered me.
He didn't seek what other have,
With joy his brow was crowned,
And loving walked the banks of Taff
As he did underground.

~~~~~~~~~~~~~~~~~

THOSE DEAR SWEET DAYS

In those dear sweet days when my Mam was young,
I remember so well all the hymns we sung,
And the saints and sinners we worshipped among,
In those dear sweet days when my Mam was young.

The pulpit, the people, the Sunday night smell
Of peppermints sucked in the teeth of hell;
The sniffers of snuff, the weak and the well,
The pulpit, the people, the Sunday night smell.

The minister preached from his closeness with God,
And even the old were unwilling to nod,
But followed the path that our Saviour trod,
As the minister preached from his closeness with God.

My Gran was contralto, so strong in the lung,
That those far from God all knew what she sung,
And were burned by Hosannahs red hot from the tongue
Of that lovely contralto so strong in the lung.

My mother was silk in a cheap cotton dress,
Work roughened flesh that I longed to caress,
Hands that could heal and lips that could bless,
Was my mother's silk in a cotton dress.

She moved through our lives like a river in flood,
Cleansing our spirits and warming our blood.
Her heart was a flower forever in bud,
As she moved through our lives like a river in flood.

My father was strength in a gentle cloak,
A battered cloth cap, and a Wild Woodbine's smoke.
A warm loving heart and a friendly joke,
Was my father's strength in a gentle cloak.

In the loom of youth with life's magic begun,
The winters were snow and the summers were sun;
Springs like champagne and the autumn's gold spun,
In the loom of youth with life's magic begun.

The white on the hills, the frost on the streets,
The ice block of time that my memory defeats,
The heart holds a vision that always repeats,
The white on the hills, the frost on the streets.

In those dear sweet days when my Mam was young
I walked on the slopes where the bluebells hung,
Where the green fern curled, where wimberry clung,
In those dear sweet days when my Mam was young.

My thanks rode high on the mountain breeze
As I saw from the crest where the hill streams freeze;
A world that was God's, and there on my knees,
My thanks rode high on the mountain breeze.

The dawns were a joy in the flame flecked sky
With the dew mist low and the cumulus high,
And they so touched my heart that I wanted to cry
With the joy of the dawn in the flame flecked sky.

I listened to speeches in Thomastown park,
To the murmur of crowds and a dog's lonely bark.
To the bumble of bees, to the lilt of the lark
As I listened to speeches in Thomastown park.

I followed the drum of the gala parade,
My mind full of dreams, my future plans made,
But how could I know that a boy's dreams can fade
As I followed the drum of the gala parade.

Through paper thin walls as I lay in my bed,
I could hear every word that our neighbours said;
No matter how secret their privacy fled
Through paper this walls as I lay in my bed.

In the dead of the night from the middle shift
The men came home from the pit and the drift,
And their dust scarred lungs took the night wind's gift,
In the dead of the night from the middle shift.

The gas lamps shone and I heard a voice,
"I am the light of the world, rejoice!
Yet I was a poor man too by choice".
And the lamps went out, but not the voice.

I blew out my candle and said a prayer
To the men in the hills and the shrouds they wear,
For I felt them around me everywhere
As I blew out my candle and said a prayer.

And there in the dark as the footsteps died,
The past and the future so mingled inside
That I knew why we laughed and knew why we cried,
In there with the dark as the footsteps died.

The stone paved hills with their fill of dead
Echoed the last of the colliers' tread,
Then settled to wait on their limestone bed,
Those stone paved hills with their fill of the dead.

The stars struck sparks from the midnight sky,
The scudding clouds made the moon's face fly,
The day had lived that the day might die,
As the stars struck sparks from the midnight sky.

In those dear sweet days when my Mam was young,
Life was a fire and death was hymn sung,
And I loved all the treasures I wandered among,
In those dear sweet days when my Mam was young.

The past rolls away as the vintage years will,
My father's at rest in the heart of a hill,
But my Mam shares our world and she's lovelier still
Though the past rolls away as the vintage years will.

And those dear sweet days, and the days to be,
Are linked by the love that she's given so free,
And I pray in my heart that she'll long comfort me,
From the days that are past to the sweet days to be.

~~~~~~~~~~~~~~~~

VANITY FREE

A friend of mine, who can hardly see,
Drove a 27 bus right into a tree,
And though it was light, he was heard to remark,
"I never did see that tree in the dark."

He never wore glasses, he really was vain,
And took no umbrella to keep off the rain.
In winter he wore the thinnest of clothes,
And icicles hung from the end of his nose.

It really was sad that his eyesight was poor,
For he slipped through a manhole into a sewer.
Vanity kills and his fall was great,
He should have worn glasses, but now it's too late.

The funeral was lovely, and out of respect,
None of the mourners wore any specs.
And a cousin called Sue and a nephew called Tim
Fell into his grave and were buried with him.

And the moral to that, if you listen to me,
Put your spectacles on if you want to see,
Or you could end up like the folk in this tale,
Vanity free but as dead as a nail!

~~~~~~~~~~~~~~~~~

I AM BUT ONE

Where lies my love in the sand of this war,
As they move to and fro with the years?
Where is the youth with a smile on his face,
Who has drowned in the flood of my tears?
Where is the joy that we constantly shared?
Where lies the grave where he rests?
"Missing in action" is all I've been told,
Just who will they say this to next?

Someone might stumble upon his poor bones,
In a field where his blood flowed in streams.
Dying for something he knew to be right,
For the honour that coloured his dreams.
Who will remember this youth if not I,
The girl who will never be wife,
Who feels she's a widow without being wed
And mourns for the rest of her life?

I am but one of these women unknown
Whose names aren't enscribed on a cross.
With no-one to tell them why love has to die,
Or share the despair of their loss.
Medals aren't struck for the ones left behind,
No silver is minted for these,
Yet they are the heroes, so brave to the end,
For they really know how to grieve.

Where lies my love in the quicksands of time,
Just where have his essences fled?
Where is the youth with a song on his lips?
Please tel me the singer's not dead.
Where are the plans that we made long ago,
The schemes that his absence have wrecked?
"Missing in action" is all I've been told,
God knows who'll be hearing this next!

~~~~

AND PASSES ON HIS WAY
(To my mother)

The morning lights the slowly turning world,
The dawning radiance floods the golden day.
The passing shades of night have held our prayers,
And God who holds the night has passed our way.

It's now that we remember what you mean,
The precious moments locked behind Time's door.
The laughing, crying wonder of it all,
The riches that we shared when we were poor.

The smell of woodsmoke in the Autumn air,
The full green hops so heavy on the bine.
The drowsy, heady, magic of the love,
That made me feel that all the world was mine.

The feel of Sunday on a summer's night,
The dusty street long shadowed by the sun,
The organ playing hymns to touch the heart,
And old, young voices fading one by one.

Our friends and neighbours, living in our dream,
A different world that will not come again.
With jazzbands marching in Cyfartha Park,
And workless miners singing in the rain.

The whinberries in bloom upon the hill,
And my dear father holding my small hand.
It happened in a world that never was,
But oh! dear God it was a happy land.

And this you gave to me, who loves you so,
And this I treasure more than priceless things.
The past is never gone while yet you live,
To share with us the joy your birthday brings.

The morning warms the slowly turning world,
The glowing radiance lights your golden day,
And God who holds the night that heard our prayers,
Saves you for us, and passes on His way.

~~~~~~~~~~~~~~~~~

THE FALL OF A SPARROW

God knows of the fall of a sparrow
And we've just lost our dear budgerigar,
And we have interred it with sorrow
By the light of the evening star.
I'm sure God knew of its passing
From the tears in our daughter's eyes,
And He will bring comfort tomorrow,
For nothing He fashions quite dies.

On the scale of a world disaster,
The death of a budgie is naught.
Yet to us and to our lovely daughter
It's not just a bird that we bought,
But a friend and a cherished companion,
Warm hearted and vibrant to touch,
Who seemed to respond to our laughter,
By shaking his feathers at us.

He is gone on the breath of a whisper,
He has flown to the nest of his dreams
With never a cry or a whimper,
Without any pain, so it seems.
And the grave out our back where he's buried,
Has a cross where our daughter still weeps,
Which is cut from the very best timber,
And shows where our Joey now sleeps.

Our Lord is aware that His creatures
All fall from their perches in turn,
And He always remembers their features
And doesn't a budgerigar spurn.
Be sure God knows of each passing
From the tears of sorrow we shed,
For to the Eternal Creator,
Nothing He fashions is dead!

" All things bright and beautiful,
   All creatures, great and small.
   All things wise and wonderful,
   The Lord God made them all.   "

~~~~~~~~~~~~~~~~~~~~~~~

TO A GRANDCHILD

Just to know you is a blessing that descends upon us all
Like a gentle mist of loving, that from the heavens fall.
We are thrilled to share your lifetime, and when happy birthdays come,
We will walk out of our darkness and will take from you the sun.

We will colour you with rainbows and polish all your days,
With shining streams of laughter and golden words of praise.
We will soothe your wounded feelings and cover tender scars
With the dewy balm of morning and night's bright cloak of stars.

We will clothe you in love's garments and wrap your nights in prayer.
Make your world a safer place by always being there.
We will thread your dreams with moonbeams as you lie so snug and warm,
That your eyes might see God's glory in the splendour of the dawn.

We will hug you in our memory as we hold you in the flesh.
Drink the words your sweet lips pour, that we may be refreshed.
Look into your lovely eyes where every precious tear
Is mirrored in a jewelled pool of all we hold most dear.

Just to see you is a blessing that the fortunate all know,
Two arms that grasp you with their power and never let you go.
A grandchild born so wonderful that we would gladly give
The essence of our lives to you, as long as you may live.

~~~~~~~~~~~~~~~~

TWENTY YEARS OR MORE

It's strange what tricks the memory plays on remembering brain.
You'd think the past would settle now, not trouble me again.
But still I see as if today those firemen I knew,
Ride the same appliances still shining bright like new.
I haven't been a fireman for twenty years or more,
But how my blood still quickens as they thunder passed my door.

I learned my craft from seasoned men at that old training school.
I climbed the tall hook ladders and stayed forever cool.
The daunting heights were naught to me, I only saw the sky,
I did what my instructors said and never reasoned why.
I haven't been a fireman for twenty years or more,
But how my spirit climbs again, as I did long ago.

I served at Cardiff, Ebbw Vale and then in Merthyr town.
Formed friendships deep, and held them long, and never was let down.
I found what men have found before, that danger draws the threads,
When flames rise high to tint the sky and walls fall passed their heads.
I haven't been a fireman for twenty years or more,
But I still see the walls fall down and hear the bright flames roar.

I never asked the world for much, what I desired was mine.
Comradeship beyond a price and hearts as warm as wine.
We rode to fires on old machines, foam tenders, pump escapes,
Converted trucks that looked like hell, with strange unearthly shapes.
I haven't been a fireman for twenty years or more,
But I still go in dreams to fires with men I can't ignore.

I met a girl from London town and joined the Service there.
Left home and friends for that true love but this I had to bear.
Yet firemen are sterling souls wherever they may be,
Their strength is steel, their friendship true, and this they gave most free.
I haven't been a fireman for twenty years or more,
But I still feel their manly love as in those days of yore.

As they flash by, I look inside the cabin where they sit,
To look for those I used to know, but now no spark is lit.
For comrades fade from Fire Brigade as new replaces old,
Though all their warmth through sharing years will never yet grow cold.
I haven't been a fireman for twenty years or more,
But how my blood still quickens as they thunder passed my door.

Perhaps one day I'll meet again those friends who shared my days,
Not in this world where men grow old but in a better place,
Where we could sit and reminisce, of smoke that scarred the lung,
And antiquated breathing sets that seemed to weight a ton.
I haven't been a fireman for twenty years or more,
But how I long to see the men who shared my life before.

I haven't been a fireman for years that form a score.
I never hear the bells go down, they sound for me no more.
I never see the friends I knew, but knocking on time's door
Come memories of golden days as glorious as before!

~~~~~~~~~~~~~~~~~

ON SWINGS AND SLIDES

I saw a boy come down a slide,
His boundless joy no cloud could hide.
'Twas like a sunset newly born,
Or else the eastern sky at dawn.

> I watched a young girl on a swing,
> Just like a bird upon the wing,
> And as her mother rocked her high,
> I'm sure I saw an angel fly.

A roundabout was spinning fast,
Young children, smiling, hurtled past.
And as these youngsters turned afresh,
They laughed out loud in happiness.

> A see-saw tipped both up and down,
> One child was white, the other brown.
> It seemed that God was showing me
> How wonderful this life could be.

And all around, on climbing frames,
Mixed coloured children played their games,
Whilst people, proud as Punch, conversed,
As parents do throughout the earth.

> For didn't He, who made the world,
> Love every boy and every girl.
> Not for the colour of their skin
> But for the souls He placed within.

He fired the sun to warm their hearts,
He lit the moon and all the stars,
To show to us that black and white
Were both as lovely in His sight.

> To me a playground seems to be
> A microscopic world set free.
> A friendly idealistic place,
> Where children learn to live in grace.

Pray God that as they grow they'll find
They haven't left such grace behind,
But will remember what was truth
On swings and slides deep in their youth.

~~~~~~~~~~~~~~~~~

HANNAH

A tribute to a brave young spirit who lit the darkness of Leeds with her love, when her beloved grandmother died.

I really like you Hannah,
You're such a lovely girl.
A sunny person like your mum,
A shining, flawless pearl.
O! how I wish more girls like you
Were born upon this earth.
How great the future then would be,
When all would know your worth.

I felt your pain in Eirwen's death,
I heard your inward cries.
The way you shared dear Sarah's loss,
The heartache and the sighs.
The way you clung in love to her,
The bond that never breaks,
And all who saw this blend of grief,
Were sad for both your sakes.

My heart went truly out to you,
Remembering the past,
When my own daughter fled this world,
For living never lasts.
It seems the day has lost its sun,
The dark devoid of stars,
As broken pieces in the heart
All bear their separate scars.

I have no doubt the day will dawn
When joy replaces loss.
For time does heal the greatest pain,
And soothe where sorrow was.
One day I know that you will be
A lovely mum and wife,
For surely He, who made us all,
Will guide you safe through life.

A wondrous future lies ahead
For special girls like you.
Your friends respect, your parents love,
Your gift for staying true.
And if Olivia has your charm,
And Elliot has your soul,
How lucky both your parents are,
For you are solid gold!

~~~~~~~~~~~~~~~~~

PAST HIS BEST

Now when my shelf life expires and I'm well past my sell by date
Embalm me with oil and wrap me in foil, then leave me outside the front gate
For I want to be recycled, not burned into ash by a flame
So I am preserved and kept in reserve, to be used all over again.

They do this at present with paper, with copper, nickel and bronze
They're all of them changed and then rearranged, without any magical wands.
My ribs could be ground into bonemeal, my fat could be rendered for soap.
While all that is sane, in the cells of my brain, could be sent in a jar to the Pope.

My hair could be stuffed into cushions, or mattresses for the elite.
My hands are adept, so they could be kept, I can't say as much for my feet.
My eyes could both be transplanted, perhaps in a dog or a cat
And most of my skin, both without and within, could be sewn in the crown of a hat.

My teeth could be made into bracelets, my tongue though inclined to be wild,
Could safely be coiled and later on boiled to make it quite tender and mild.
So now that my shelf life's expiring, and younger folk stacked in my place
Embalm and preserve me, though you don't deserve me,
                            and stamp "Past his best" on my face!

~~~~~~~~~~~~~~~~~

ANGEL OF GOD

I sat on a mountain, barren of love,
Dreaming the long golden hours away,
When out of the mist that fell from above,
I saw a light and heard a voice say,
"I am a messenger sent from on high,
Angel of God with a tale to tell,
Rouse from your slumber while I show you why
The road you tread is the way to hell!"

"I'll make you an offer you can't refuse,
(So said this Angel Of God to me)
It's called the Gospel and it means good news,
For you'll live in Heaven, eternally.
It isn't for sale, no matter the price,
For One has paid with the blood He shed.
Repent and believe and this will suffice".
(And this was all that the angel said).

I read my bible where Matthew began,
(The dust flew fast from the opened book,)
And I learned the truth of God made man,
His lowly birth and the road He took.
I trod in His footsteps from Matthew to John,
(O! what a joy and a thrill that was),
Sharing the love and the glory that shone
From Bethlehem's star to Calvary's cross.

I sat on my mountain through sun and rain,
Praying God's angel would once more speak.
Spent many hours but waited in vain,
(How time dragged on that lonely peak).
I had found the Way, the Truth and the Life,
For the Gospel signs were plain to see.
But needed a guide on the road to Christ,
And my angel friend was this to me.

Then I heard a voice on the evening air,
Like streams of praise from a golden horn,
Which so thrilled my soul as I waited there,
I knew I was of the spirit born.
The Word that came filled my cup to the brim,
The path I shared was the one Christ trod,
I needed no angel to show me Him,
For the voice itself came straight from God.

Yes, straight from God came that awesome sound,
(Oh! how uplifted my soul became),
And I fell to my knees on that sacred ground,
As the King of Heaven recited my name.
Now I am a messenger sent from Him,
Angel Of Light with a tale to tell.
Rouse from your slumber, repent your sin,
Or the road you tread is the way to hell!

~~~~~~~~~~~~~~~~~

MONSTERS

In the world of little children
There are monsters to be seen.
Giant shapes and hideous shadows
That are bloated and obscene.
From recesses in their cradles,
Through the bars of wooden cots,
Male and female great Goliaths
Scare the pants off tiny tots.

In the world of mums and daddies
There are midgets everywhere.
Little elves and tiny fairies
Tucked up tight or strapped in chairs.
They are fed by breast or bottle,
They are served strained soup from Heinz,
And some are little terrors
Who will grow quite large in time.

And the monsters seen by children
As they look up from the floor,
Are simply both their parents
Coming through a giant door.
While the midgets, elves and fairies
That we dads and mummies see
Are tiny tots, scared half to death
By giants such as we.

~~~~~~~~~~~~~~~~~

EPITAPH FOR A MINER

I would be a wild, free songbird,
If I could but live again.
Beat my wings where sighing leaves stirred,
Through the days of sun and rain.
See my world from heights of sweet joy,
Not from depths of bitter pain,
A bird I'd be and not a boy,
If I could but live again.

I would sing in swaying green trees,
If I could but sing once more.
To sweet wild flowers and fat striped bees,
And the hawks that proudly soar.
I wouldn't breathe the grimy coal dust,
Mocking fly through pit cage door,
But I would sing as free birds must,
If I could but sing once more.

I would sit on terrace chimney,
Feel the blazing warmth of coal,
See my old friends going grimly,
Down Man's black, lung pitting, hole.
I would hear their anxious wives speak,
From stark fear within the soul,
Hopeful signs see, that their eyes seek,
Where torn earth exacts its toll.

I would strut the cowslip meadows,
Quench my thirst from trout clean brooks.
Chase the long midsummer shadows,
Through fern sprayed, sequestered nooks.
I would peck fat seeds from furrows,
When the ploughman absent looks,
Gather fur from rabbit burrows,
For my nest amidst the rooks.

I would not hop, free, on slagheap,
Graceful skim the pithead wheel;
Sing requiem where collier dead sleeps,
Past the twisted rails of steel.
I would not drop twigs on graveyards,
Flap my wings where mourner kneels,
Swoop to read the flowered grey cards,
Where sad words the heart reveals.

I would not go where the wind blow,
Through that shattered pane of glass,
I would not look through that window,
Where I watched the seasons pass.
I would not do this from duty,
Life burns like the summer grass,
I would yet remember beauty,
Where the ivy creepers mass.

I would be a wild free songbird,
If I could but live again.
I would know the love the soul stirred,
Through the days of sun and rain.
I'd see stars through dew drenched green leaves,
Not from shafts of deep mined pain,
A bird I'd be, not man who grieves,
If I could but live again!

~~~~~~~~~~~~~~~~~

THE HEALING SIDE OF MARRIAGE

On the grown-up side of childhood, when you both are left alone
When every daughter, every son, has fled the family home,
There are silences in corners, there are many empty chairs,
A dearth of ringing laughter that once wiped away dull care.
The radio plays ballads now but deep within the soul
You long to hear your children as they sang to rock and roll.
The bedroom doors still bear their names and as you go inside,
You seem to see them standing there in all their youthful pride.
The air vibrates with echoed words, the walls their shadows fold
Whilst legacies of tender smiles wind round a core of gold.
Then all at once the feeling comes that time is but a stream
Where you can't swim against the flow to live again your dreams.
As you face a lonely future and your sorrows fall like rain,
The grown-up side of childhood comes, to haunt your heart again.

On the healing side of marriage, when all your fears are stilled,
As one by one, grandchildren come, and empty hearts are filled.
There's a sense of better times to come, where life's again worthwhile
A burnishing of clouded hopes with every baby smile.
You share each crowded day of joy, as swift each infant grows,
Remembering the other times so very long ago,
When children in the home were yours and you were setting out
To make for them a brave new world unmarred by fear or doubt.
Now this gives way to other dreams that all grandparents share,
That they will live to see the day when their granddaughter wears
A wedding ring of purest gold, a bridal gown of white,
A flowered posy in her hands and eyes that shine so bright
That all are dazzled by her smile and moved deep in the soul,
As the healing side of marriage comes, to bring her joy untold!

~~~~~~~~~~~~~~~~~

IT WAS A CHILD

One fearful night ('twas Halloween)
The ghost of childhood past was seen,
And as folk looked into its face,
They lost their faith and fell from grace.

No questions of this ghoul were asked,
We knew it not, for it was masked
But thought it was, a child of Pan,
Who never grew into a man.

It stayed to walk each city street
To scare all those it chanced to meet,
As priests and laymen old and wise
Tried in their turn to exorcise.

But this all proved beyond their power,
It still befouled the midnight hour.
So as in sleep the townsfolk tossed,
They woke to find their souls were lost.

It was an evil town by then
Paraded by the ghosts of men
Who as the frightful lanes they trod
Had no belief or faith in God.

It was a child who saved us all
A baby born in cattle stall
A child in swaddling clothes arrayed
And in a manger gently laid.

For Christmas day had come at last
To lay the ghost of childhood past
For as the Christ child came to save
The ghoul departed to its grave.

One happy night ('twas Christmas Eve)
The Holy Spirit on us breathed;
And as we looked into His face,
We found our faith and walked in grace!

~~~~~~~~~~~~~~~~

IF I WERE

If I were a gambling man, then I would only bet
Those silver coins I could afford, and not get into debt,
For I have seen men brought so low in this and other lands,
That they'd surrender all they own to give up games of chance.

If I were a drinking man, then drunk I'd never be,
For I would not let liquor take such a strong hold on me.
I would not let it ruin those who share with me this life,
The children whom I still adore, or my sweet, lovely, wife.

If I were a foolish man, like many other mugs
Who poison blood and rot the brain with soul-destroying drugs,
Then I would walk the road to hell, yet pray that I would find
The strength to leave this filth alone, from somewhere in my mind.

If I were a widowed man, although I'd make new friends,
Another wife I'd never take, I'm hers 'til this life ends.
But she would not want me to be beyond love's endless reach,
And I would seek companionship, so she could rest in peace.

If I were a violent man, then I would pray to God
To make me change my brutish ways, and follow where Christ trod,
To ask forgiveness from all those whose lives I once destroyed,
For if I could redeem myself then I'd be overjoyed.

O! Let me be a gentle man, I don't ask more than this.
A home wherein my honour dwells, and my wife's lips to kiss.
Arms to hold a grandchild close, with prayer to cleanse my soul,
And love beyond all earthly dreams, to crown my life with gold!

~~~~~~~~~~~~~~~~

WHERE THE TREE OF LOVING GREW

There used to be no colour in the darkest mining vales
There used to be no singing like the kind that's heard in Wales.
Now is it any wonder with the comradeship we knew
That we lived for one another where the tree of loving grew.

There used to be no football like the games our village played
There used to be no pitches quite as steep or badly laid.
Our jerseys all were faded and our hands and feet were numb
But we ran opponents ragged as we beat them one by one.

There used to be no chapel like the one we knew so well,
There used to be no preacher like the one who gave us hell,
But though he preached of brimstone, his whole soul was filled with grace
And we knew his Maker loved him from the glory on his face.

There used to be no water like the stream in which we swam,
There used to be no scolding like the kind we got from Mam.
We tore our shirts and trousers knowing well that we would pay
With yet another hiding at the closing of the day.

There used to be no toffee like the kind my sisters made
The flavour was delicious for it was their stock in trade.
They poured it into cake tins making toffee dabs galore
Then sold them for a penny each instead of charging more.

There used to be no market like the one in Pontypridd,
The peas would belch and bubble and the faggots all would seethe.
We sat down and enjoyed them though our stomachs filled with gas,
Then walked around contended for we knew the pain would pass.

There used to be the whip and top and marbles in a ring
Bows and arrows crudely made and kites upon a string.
Skipping ropes for boys and girls and hopscotch in the street,
O! how I still remember all those tiny dancing feet.

There isn't any picture now like films we used to see
Sometimes we paid a penny and sometimes we stole in free.
Our cowboys all were heroes and our Indians all were bad,
As I rode into the sunset on the shoulders of my dad.

We hadn't lost our innocence or found that life was dust,
We rolled foul mountain herbs for fags and smoked then with disgust.
We talked about the universe O! we were grownup then!
We wore our first long trousers and we thought that we were men.

It isn't very likely now that I will know the joy,
The bittersweet fulfilment that was part of that small boy.
Sometimes I cry in silence knowing childhood cannot last
And dream of all the golden days I knew of in the past.

~~~~~~~~~~~~~~~~~

LILIAN AND GRACE

Two grand old ladies who live door to door,
Sisters and widows for ten years or more.
Caring and sharing and fine as old lace,
A joy to behold are sweet Lilian and Grace.

I meet them out shopping when Friday comes round
Quietly happy, their lives firmly bound.
They speak without malice, their joy plain to see,
Making the day so much brighter for me.

They both love their dancing, Sequence, Old Time,
Taking each other and blending like wine.
Waltzes and Saunters, Rumbas and Blues,
Nimble and quick in their silvery shoes.

Talking to folk as they walk round the hall,
Laughing and waving and having a ball.
Shaking the hands of their sociable friends,
Who smile their farewells as the dancing night ends.

Back to their homes and a cold lonely bed,
Dreaming perhaps of the day they were wed.
Of husbands and children who shared happy days
As they walked through the years with Lilian and Grace.

Through every bereavement they both share the grief
Supporting each other, their love running deep.
The flame of their lives burns so bright in the soul
The warmth that surrounds them will never grow cold.

Two grand old ladies who live side by side,
Sisters and widows since their husbands died.
Comrades in arms for they're never apart,
As loving they build a new home in the heart.

~~~~~~~~~~~~~~~~

THE ALIEN

I looked at the huge ghastly monster,
    Who came to invade my domain.
Writhing great feelers grew out of its fur
    But never the sign of a brain.
A sphere of white with fungus around
    Was balanced on top of its mass,
With mouth like a drain where my family could drown
    And voice like the bray of an ass.

Feelers came down where my relatives live,
    Another came down in my hole.
To the end of my days I'll never forgive,
    This treacherous, barbarous soul.
Without even knowing he made us all squirm,
    As only these foul creatures can;
For we are a nest of unfortunate worms,
    While he is the beast of a man!

~~~~~~~~~~~~~~~~

COAL IS NEVER CLEAN

There isn't any beauty in the job of mining coal.
There isn't any lifting of the spirit in the soul.
There isn't any sweetness in the mind or in the lung,
But only dust and danger for the old and for the young.

There isn't any work's canteen deep down within the pit.
No sign of any tables or a chair on which to sit.
No ladies wheeling trollies bearing tea and fancy cakes,
But only miles of rutted rails and noise a coal truck makes.

There isn't much of comfort found where darkness reigns supreme,
Not when there's deadly pressure on the upright and the beam.
There isn't anywhere to run or place in which to hide,
When all the world falls down on you and something breaks inside.

The social graces aren't observed where toil is muck and sweat.
There isn't talk of Ladies Day at Ascot and the rest.
Of Eton, Harrow, Winchester or other Public Schools,
Not when there's scars upon the skin and blood upon the tools.

There isn't sun or stars to see, or breezes that are fresh.
You'll never see a changing sky or feel the wind's caress.
It's either freezing cold or hot and dirt that seems obscene,
For coal is master down below and coal is never clean.

It isn't that the men complain, they know within the soul,
You either labour in the dark or languish on the Dole.
They only wish with all their hearts that those who scorn their name,
Would come and share a single shift before they next defame.

No! beauty's always absent when the coal is cut and trimmed.
And darkness comes into its own when safety lamps are dimmed.
But there is always comradeship, a fire kept burning bright
For men can't help but see the flame where day is always night!

~~~~~~~~~~~~~~~~~~~~~~~

DANNY

Danny was a man who walked through hell,
His wind scorched face forever wreathed in smiles.
Danny was a friend who knew you well,
And shared your griefs along life's lonely miles.
Danny was a force that turned aside,
The buffetings that fate so harshly dealt.
Danny was a man who held inside
The anger that at times he must have felt.

Danny was a person, poor in health,
And yet through suff'ring took your hurts away.
Danny's was the good that worked through stealth,
The brightest corner of the darkest day.
Danny was a feeling in the mind,
A healing blend, compassionate and sweet.
Danny was the heart of all mankind,
Eternal good no evil can defeat.

Danny was companion to the poor,
In friendship sharing dignity with them.
Danny was the rock forever sure,
The very last to point and to condemn.
Danny was the symbol of the past,
That learned to give without a thought of gain,
Danny's life was over much too fast,
A brief encounter with the knives of pain.

Danny is a name we can't forget,
Though he who bore it, lies within a hill.
Danny was the finest man I met,
And buried laughter comes to cheer me still.
Danny was a footstep in the hall,
Two hands that held my cheeks in gentleness.
Danny was a photo on the wall,
A generous mouth that smiled with tenderness.

Danny was my father, staunch and true,
A bunch of curls that fell across a brow.
Danny was the man we listened to,
And my heart aches to listen to him now.
Danny was a person overjoyed,
To share with us his world beneath the hill,
Danny is in his grave in Cefn Coed,
But mourn him not, for he is with us still.

And Danny speaks when words of comfort flow,
And Danny laughs when our own children smile,
And Danny walks where'er our footsteps go,
And Danny's mem'ry stays with us a while.
The Merthyr valley weeping goes its way,
The brooding hillsides rising like a wall,
The sleeping sun awaits the dawning day,
And Danny shines, sublime, above them all.

~~~~~~~~~~~~~~~~~

THE PILGRIM PEACE

I went by thought to Ulster, dear God! why did I go,
When O! so many hawks and doves had flown that way before.
I didn't go a protestant, or from the Church of Rome,
But simply as the pilgrim peace, who longed to find a home.

I came to Londonderry, dear God! why did I come?
It wasn't for proud orangemen who marched behind a drum.
It wasn't for Republicans, or for the I.R.A,
But simply for the end of war, and dawn of Christian day.

I travelled on to Belfast, dear God! was this the place?
To where the angel Satan came when he fell far from grace.
The flowering flames from petrol bombs lit up the old Falls road,
But no-one thought to look past hate to where God's mercy flowed.

I came at last to Stormont, dear God! did hope die here?
As Ian Paisley's angry words created clouds of fear.
I didn't come for bigotry, I didn't bear a grudge,
I travelled here to weigh the facts, before I chanced to judge.

And so I offer up this prayer, dear God! show forth your power.
Make lion now lie down with lamb, this surely is the hour.
For Ulster isn't Protestant, or yet the Church of Rome,
But simply where the Pilgrim Peace, has yet to find a home!

~~~~~~~~~~~~~~~~~

TOO OLD FOR TOYS

I let my eyes feast on the pride of the beast,
As it trotted with fire 'round the ring.
A fine circus horse, bright be-ribboned of course,
And as gay as a bird on the wing.
A star spangled rider, bareback, was astride her,
But the beast was the star of the show,
And the ribbons did fly, as she tossed her head high,
With the dust of the ring far below.

I looked at my daughter, and thought then I caught her,
With the back of her hand brushing tears,
That unbidden had flowed, down the cheeks that had glowed,
With the fervour of ten tender years.
We came from the city, where I out of pity,
Had brought her along to the show,
Where the horses she loved, pushed, jostled, and shoved,
As around the arena they'd go.

She was too young for boys, and was too old for toys,
Though she longed for the gift of a foal;
But horses need pasture, warm straw, and a master,
And this was like gall to her soul.
My heart had to harden, our flat had no garden,
No space for a young horse to run;
And though she would grieve, with her heart on her sleeve,
There was nothing on earth to be done.

So I let her eyes feast on the pride of the beast,
And I hoped at the end of the show,
That the memory gained would still be retained,
As we trudged our way home through the snow.
But though truth may burn, all the young have to learn,
That life is for living it seems,
That our childhood must pass, as it withers like grass,
Though still kept alive in our dreams.

~~~~~~~~~~~~~~~~~

A MOTHER IS

A mother is a memory from the past,
A mother is today with all its love,
A mother is a vision that will last
Until we meet again in Heaven above.

A mother is a heart that always cares,
A mother is two arms that held me tight,
A mother is a smile enchantment wears,
That fades not with the day but lights the night.

A mother is the crown we children place
Above the brow that only thinks of us,
A mother is a spirit dressed in grace
That dances on the wings we know as trust.

A mother is a tear from worry's eye
As she in sorrow shares our pain and grief,
A mother is a message from on high
That binds us with chains of our belief.

A mother is an ever flowing stream
That rises in the mountains that are gold,
Then tumbles from the day into a dream
That forms a pool of joy within the soul.

A mother is the seed our Saviour sows,
It matters not how barren is the earth;
For from this seed the loveliest flower grows
And only we can ever know its worth.

A mother is a concept thought by god
When this dear world was fashioned long ago.
A mother is the road our Saviour trod,
A mother is the debt we'll always owe.

A mother is embracingly the light
That changes dark to daytime with its kiss,
Then makes us kneel in prayer within the night
To offer thanks for all a mother is!

~~~~~~~~~~~~~~~~~

NO FUTURE

All that is gone has an ending,
All of the present will pass.
Its no good we mortals pretending
That we'll live forever, alas!
This planet will keep on revolving,
The rain and the snow will still fall,
The sun, moon and stars are eternal,
But man has no future at all!

~~~~~~~~~~~~~~~~~

I WAS YOUNG THEN

I was young then, just another boy,
Who laughed, and cried, and played as all boys do.
Drank from springs of gladness, warmth and joy,
And fed upon the only world I knew.

I was free then, on unfenced mountainside,
And I could run till heart could pump no more,
Rivers to swim and mountain horse to ride,
And books to swop with friends who lived next door.

I was foolish then, for boys see but the game,
And whilst I played the workday world rolled on,
Dropped all my studies, lessons seemed so tame,
And woke to find the golden schooldays gone.

I was chapel then, and in the Boys' Brigade,
Dear God! was I that lad in black and white?
If that were me, when did the brightness fade,
And was my daytime mortgaged to the night?

I was happy then, my cup filled to the brim,
The future called, but I was just content
To run the roads, to climb, to idly swim,
And count with friends the happy hours we spent.

I was sheltered then, by parents dear and true,
Loved from the heart and cradled to the soul,
Cried over, laughed with, bad and good days through,
And found restored the joys the grey days stole.

I am grateful now, though time has passed me by,
And when my friends bemoan advancing age,
I open up life's book that riches cannot buy,
Read what has gone, and turn another page.

I have finished now, but only for this day,
Behold the endless vistas, bright before my door.
There will be tears shed, but in my heart I pray,
That I will live my life and never ask for more.

~~~~~~~~~~~~~~~~

LITTLE DANIEL

Little Daniel, eight last April,
Is a very happy boy,
Living in some railway coaches,
Every day is filled with joy.
All around him, on wood sleepers,
Rusty rails run through the grass,
To great engine sheds whose windows
Watch the world through broken glass.

Once he lived in some great city,
Cheek by jowl with smoke and grime.
High rise buildings, like brick boxes,
In a vast, unbroken line.
School was like a paupers prison,
Bars on windows, concrete floors.
Asphalt paving in the playground,
Bolts and locks on all the doors.

Little Daniel, nine next birthday,
Was a frightened boy back then.
Bullied by his lumpish elders,
Who had made his childhood hell.
Threatened for his dinner money,
Forced to part with treasured gifts.
Sometimes beaten without reason,
Badly marked by bruising fists.

Both his parents earned their living
In some menial, ill-paid job.
Trapped it seems within a system,
Where it paid to cheat or rob.
Though they yearned for something better,
This, it seemed, would never come.
Folk like them were always losers,
Born to live in some foul slum.

Little Daniel prayed each evening
For his parents and himself.
Didn't plead for something lavish,
Didn't pray for endless wealth.
Asked instead for God to give them
Only that which was enough.
Some clean place where they could settle,
Some warm home that they could love.

Like a searing flash of lightening,
Like a thunderbolt from God,
Came an offer to his parents,
Of a home and of a job.
Some small-holding in the country,
With a place to lay their heads.
'Though 'twas but some railway coaches
Set amidst great engine sheds.

Little Daniel has a birthday
Every morn when he awakes.
All around him lies the country,
Rolling hills and placid lakes.
For he helps his parents manage
Fields of produce, pigs and hens.
Breathing air so fresh and healthy,
Far from where the city ends.

There's a moral to this story,
Dream your dreams though life be grim.
Kneel before God's throne each evening,
Offer up your prayers to Him.
You could be like little Daniel
Eight last April, nine next year,
Yet have birthdays every morning,
If you do what I ask here!

~~~~~~~~~~~~~~~~~

IN BRECONSHIRE

In Breconshire my true love lies,
Where mountain ramparts heavenward rise,
And soft blown ferns like angel sighs,
Rest light as shadows on her eyes.

We walked into the morning, where,
We saw the dancing grass prepare,
From that sweet flower abounding there,
A daisy chain to crown her hair.

The dawn a golden touch away,
God's afternoon across the way,
The evening tucked beyond the day,
Night's bed prepared where children pray.

These were the glorious hours for me,
Before death set her spirit free,
And now in dreams and reverie,
I touch her hand in memory.

When she was with me, shadows fled,
While summer hung from spring's bright thread,
And goodness flowed through all she said,
To inward dry the tears unshed.

It was as if her mind could feel,
The wildflowers crush beneath her heel,
Or know the stab through heart of steel,
Or hear a beggar's mute appeal.

Some magic quality she had,
That touched the soul that once was sad,
To strengthen good and heal the bad,
And make the downcast spirit, glad.

These joys can't fade as shadows must,
The golden hours can never rust,
Reality outlives the dust,
Immortal beats the heart we trust.

In Breconshire my true love sleeps,
Where soft winds sigh, and willows weep,
Where sky it's cloudy harvest reaps,
And earth, it's joyous burden, keeps.

~~~~~~~~~~~~~~~~

SWEETHEART FOREVER

A wife is a sweetheart forever,
A wife is the essence of truth.
Sharing and caring together,
The girl that you loved in your youth.
No person alive could replace her,
She burns through your blood like a flame,
And when in your joy you embrace her,
You bless the sweet day that she came.

No power or person could change her,
So steadfastly brave to the end.
She came to you once as a stranger,
And stayed to be lover and friend.
Each moment you share is fulfilling,
Each touch of her hand is divine,
Whilst the taste of her lips is so thrilling,
That living and life are sublime.

The babies she bears are your treasure,
The jewels that make up your crown,
You love every child beyond measure,
And hope that you won't let them down.
One day she will be a grandmother,
And O, what a great one she'll be,
For she gives of herself like no other,
And shares of this loving most free.

A wife is a stranger no longer
A wife is a light in the gloom,
Her feelings grow warmer and stronger,
A flower forever in bloom.
So you thank the eternal Creator
For the gift that he brought to your door,
And you know as you kiss and embrace her,
She will live in your heart evermore.

~~~~~~~~~~~~~~~~

BACHGEN BACH
(Little Boy)

Well, Bachgen Bach, you've seen it all,
Why wait 'til you grow old.
You've heard the bugle's morning call,
You've watched the day grow cold.
The winter snow has touched your cheek,
Your eyes have looked past spring,
And there in summer, Autumn waits,
To see what youth will bring.

You've walked the roads the Romans' made,
You've heard their ghostly tread,
And there as echoed footsteps fade,
You've marched amidst the dead.
Immortal hills where Normans fought,
Now live as darkness falls,
But you have found what conquerors sought,
Beyond their castle walls.

The ironworks have long since gone,
You've played where steelworks rust.
You've heard the nest birds joyous song,
You've breathed the slagheaps dust.
Life's images before your eyes,
Have flickered, flared and flown,
The weak, the strong, the fools, the wise,
The Queen upon her throne.

There's nothing left in life to see,
Your collier father's dead.
His rock hard lungs have set him free,
And stained your mother's bed.
Beneath your feet the black earth sinks,
As falls fill empty shafts,
While in the pubs the miner drinks,
And laughs his mirthless laughs.

You've seen the waste that clogs the streams,
The hills the pits made dark.
On summer days you've dreamed your dreams,
On benches in the park.
You've looked around at old men there,
With winter in their eyes;
Past dreaming now, they sit and stare,
Until the long day dies.

Why wait for this, child of my land,
There's nothing left but age.
Life holds not more to understand,
Flee now this valley cage.
Beyond that mountain, grass is green,
And trout in bright streams lie.
Go find the Wales that God keeps clean,
Let not youth's freshness die.

Well, Bachgen bach, live now your hopes,
Though times be bittersweet.
Ascend the sunlit upland slopes,
With wings to lift your feet.
A prince of Wales you are my boy,
Why wait 'til you grow old.
Through this dear land go thou in joy,
Unto the hills of gold.

~~~~~~~~~~~~~~~~

JESTERS ALL

Time must pass and mortals change,
Death is funny, living, strange.
Across the hours jokes are writ,
And jesters all in judgement sit.

The human comedy goes on,
While masks on clowns are put upon.
And there beneath the painted face,
In fools disguise, the human race.

The belly laugh, the bawdy pun,
The emptiness behind the fun.
Up front the smiles, backstage the pain,
For comics all must jest again.

If there be someone wise enough,
To sit in judgement up above,
Then surely bolts of fire will fall,
To sear our souls and burn us all.

We play a kind of hopscotch game,
And hop from war to war and maim,
With atom bombs and not with mirth,
Our fellow sharers of the earth.

If there be hope, and we must pray,
that tortured night gives way to day,
Then it is this, that children grow,
While ageing jesters come and go.

I like to think the young will find
An answer that will save mankind,
Then, throwing clownish masks away,
Will fashion love from mortal clay.

The world is but a circus ring,
Where children laugh and joy is king.
Where beasts are tamed and tightly caged,
And vast extravaganza staged.

The tinsel glitters 'neath the lights,
The flesh is warm within the tights.
The horses circle as they run,
Just like our world around the sun.

The big tent is the universe,
And people specks of dust, or worse.
While we who clap, and those who star,
Know deep inside how small we are.

The Great Ringmaster cracks His whip,
The constallations wheel and dip.
This can we hope that through the pain,
We'll find our world reborn again.

~~~~~~~~~~~~~~~~~~

JUNK MAIL

They come through my door by the sackful,
The leaflets, the offers of gain.
Each one of them brash and not bashful,
Again, and again, and again.
In a week they amount to a hillock,
In a month they're a mountainous mass,
These people must think me a pillock
To accept all this terrible trash.

The offers on house double glazing
I have made a conservatory from;
And though you might think this amazing,
The structure is simple, yet strong.
The prize money draws I'm receiving
From firms like The Readers Digest
Have all of my family believing
I'm building my own treasure chest.

Firms offer to clean all my carpets
With foam that just loves to eat dust.
There's leaflets from three supermarkets
With prices that leave me nonplussed.
Fat catalogues filled up my hallway
Sometimes I can't open the door
I must be the world's biggest wally,
There must be a hundred or more.

I have just opened up the Informer
And dozens of adverts fell out.
From Somerfields, Great Mills and Saunas,
Who all for my services tout.
My letter box I have cemented,
A mantrap's in place by my gate
And though you might think I'm demented
Myself, I am feeling just great.

I have had a long phone call from Wendy
A clerk at a Chapel of Rest
Who has a prospectus to send me
Of thirty-two coffins no less.
I will soak this farrago in petrol,
Then push it alight through her door
And though it won't burn all the metal
The chapel and coffins should go.

My lounge is now packed to the ceiling
With charity begging appeals.
And newspapers coyly concealing
Brochures for take-away meals.
I have asked for three skips and an artic
A trailer and furniture van,
To clear the junk mail from my attic
And flush every page down the pan.

It seems I'm a sucker for junk mail,
The word has gone 'round I'm a mug.
The easiest person to blackmail
If you have a product to plug.
But for those who still think me too placid
I have dug a great moat 'round my house
And when I have filled it with acid,
I'll prove I'm a man, not a mouse!

~~~~~~~~~~~~~~~~

THOSE GOLDEN DAYS

Where have my childhood memories flown?
Those golden days spent in the sun.
The simple pleasures I have known,
When all my world was fresh and young.

Where are the hopscotch playing girls
Who jumped and danced on numbered squares?
Where are the skipping ropes they twirled,
Where fade the ribbons from their hair?

Those round and marvellous bullseye sweets
That changed in colour on the tongue.
The mint imperial Sunday treats
We sucked in church when hymns were sung.

Where are the penny sugar mice,
Both pink and white with eyes like jade?
The tiger nuts, the liquorice pipes,
The toffee dabs our sisters made.

Those graceful, coloured, homemade kites
That swooped and soared in every breeze.
The nettle stings, the insect bites,
The knuckled ham and mushy peas.

Where are the barley sugar sticks
That twisted upright in their jars?
The bags of sherbert that we licked,
The clockwork trains and racing cars.

The picture palaces of old
The penny rush on Saturdays.
When our drab world was changed to gold,
Before our rapt, enchanted gaze.

Where are the stockings that we hung
With such bright hopes on Christmas Eve?
The lovely carols that were sung
So long ago, when we believed.

The curling tongues our sisters used,
To make them look like movie stars.
The scented water that they brewed
From roses crushed in old jam jars.

Where now the jerseys that we wore
With coloured stripes around the chest?
The flannel trousers seen no more,
The cotton shorts, the itchy vest.

Those ancient tramcars in the streets
That jerked and jumped on rutted rails.
The polished, slatted, wooden seats
That always seemed as hard as nails.

Where are the tips down which we slid
On crazy things we used as sleighs?
Like some discarded saucepan lid
Or mams unwanted metal trays.

The outings that our chapel ran
To Barry Island or Pontsarn.
The seven arches graceful span
Or castles built on golden sand.

Where grows the hopfields of our youth,
The flowering bines of brilliant green?
The dreams we dreamed when life was truth
And all the world was sweet and clean.

Our family around a fire
Of flaming logs or glowing coke.
The sprays of hops on rusty wire,
Remembered faces, wreathed in smoke.

Is there a temple deep in time
That still retains such joy as this?
And is there stored within that shrine
A father's strength, a mother's kiss.

Where do such lovely people go?
Where burn such beacons through the night?
Where are the folk who loved us so?
Where fold the arms that held us tight?

Where sings my gran to me again,
Those lovely hymns we harmonized?
Where lies my grandad's bed of pain?
Where are the sons he idolised?

Their pleasures always seemed enough,
For him an ounce of Pigtail Twist.
For her a pinch of menthol snuff,
And happy games of knockout whist.

Where are the collier buses gone?
That shook and rattled to the mine.
And do they still take colliers on
To some great coalfield deep in time?

Where is the chapel where we met
To worship God and sing His praise?
Do we remember or forget
The love we shared in happier days?

My mother's arms so rough and red
From washtub, soap and scrubbing board.
The lumpy, mattressed, brass framed bed
Where I was born and hope restored.

Where are the duties that were hers?
The Sisterhood and Girls Brigade.
The good fight fought through bitter years,
The uniforms, the church parade.

Where are the bikes we used to ride
Down valley roads on threadbare tyres?
As we pressed onward in our pride,
Passed pithead wheels and chapel spires.

Mouthorgan music, sad but sweet
That thrilled the senses, touched the soul.
Played by old miners in the street,
Who were, perchance, upon the Dole.

Where are the leapfrog jumping boys,
Who seemed to spring so fast and high?
Where are the gaudy Woolworth's toys,
That our dear parents used to buy?

The skipping ropes we used to twirl,
The whips that spun each wooden top.
The endless, teeming childhood whirl
That we once thought would never stop.

Where are the blizzards that would fill
The terraced streets with drifting snow?
As we made sleigh rides from each hill
Descend into the town below.

Those headlong rushes down each slope
On makeshift sleds that fell apart.
Their runners greased with Sunlight soap
And oiled by joy from every heart.

Where are the hoops we ran behind,
Where are the ancient tyres we rolled?
Where are our friends so warm and kind,
Where are the hands we used to hold?

The tender girls in Sunday frocks,
Their wayward hair in frizzy plaits.
In shiny shoes and cotton socks
And rakish tam-o-shanter hats.

Where are the hordes of little boys
Who ragged ran down mountainside?
To fill the valley with their noise
Until the evening shadows dies.

The social evenings in our church
With Postman's Knock our favourite game.
To kiss as if our hearts would burst,
Before the age of reason came.

Where fades the mystery of time?
Where dims the lifeforce in the eye?
Where are the glowing dawns sublime?
Where did such endless promise die?

O! loving Lord, could we return
To where such innocence awaits,
Then surely we would evil spurn
And walk once more through childhood's gates!

~~~~~~~~~~~~~~~~

IN YOUR INFINITE MERCY

Can we say we're a civilized nation
As we witness the beast in Man.
Abusing poor innocent children,
In every foul way that he can.
Infants are shook and then beaten,
Young boys are the prey of old men,
While girls hardly out of their cradles,
Will never know childhood again.

O God! in your infinite mercy,
Bring all your compassion to bear
On the minds and the hearts of people
Who seem so unable to care.
Make every child safe from molesters,
Let boys grow to manhood unstained,
Make honour and trust a great barrier,
So girls become women unchanged.

I look in the eyes of grandchildren,
To see in their innocent depths
The joy that is there for the taking,
If only we show them respect.
As we walk hand in hand to the future,
Where faith in their destiny lies,
We know we are privileged people
For love such as this never dies.

In a world that is full of distinctions,
Let's concentrate minds on this truth,
That we're failing the next generation
Unless they are cherished in youth.
The people who lead us tomorrow
Are babes who but wait to be born,
Let's banish the dark that precedes them
So they can arrive in the dawn!

~~~~~~~~~~~~~~~~~

YESTERDAY'S FIRE

It's not easy to sum up a brother,
Or sister, in words that are new.
But how to describe a Mother
In words that are tender and true?
How can you speak of a lifetime of love,
In phrases that roll off the tongue,
Or praise a wonderful woman enough
When you think of the things she has done.
Of the toil and the hardship she suffered,
Of the pain and the grief that she bore,
Of the comfort and solace she offered
In the days that we shared long ago.

It comes to me now like a knife thrust,
The worry that my mother knew.
The way that she laboured with love and trust,
Although the rewards were so few.
In two tiny rooms we were housed and fed,
But they seemed like a palace to me.
I never thought of the tears that were shed
In places where we couldn't see.
But oh! how my heart now remembers,
And oh! how my eyes still retain,
A vision of time's glowing embers
From yesterday's fire of pain.
And mam I will love you forever,
Not only on each Mother's Day,
And pray that we'll journey together
Where fountains of happiness play.

~~~~~~~~~~~~~~~~

THIS WONDERFUL FATHER OF YOURS

A father is strength when his children are weak, gentleness when they are hurt.
Enthroned in their hearts from the time they are born, a king in an open neck shirt.
Someone who runs with a ball at his feet, to show how a game should be played,
Then bolsters resolve with a steadying hand all those times when they're feeling afraid.
His stories at bedtime to help you to sleep, a kiss on a brow that is warm,
A haven of peace, where you anchor your soul, in the dark of a gathering storm.

A father is energy biding its time, a dynamo humming with power,
A build-up of pressure that waits to erupt, destiny coming to flower.
He holds in his grasp all his family's hopes, he squeezes them dry of their fear,
He raises their spirits, smiles through his pain and brushes away every tear.
He works with his brain or maybe his brawn, not always a pleasure to him,
Through long weary hours and desolate days, 'till the light in his eyes grows dim.

A father is laughter that echoes through time, merriment filling the home.
Strong arms that will nurse you when you are a child, a hug and a kiss when
you're grown.
Someone who worries when illness befalls, then patiently waits through the night,
Hiding his grief until he's alone, for men have to cry out of sight.
He's strength when it's needed and gentleness too, a blend of the bitter and sweet,
A foundation stone for the hearth and the home, a force that no evil defeats.

A father is someone who feels no regret when the years blend his hair to grey,
His greatest reward is an upturned face he can kiss at the end of the day.
When children leave home, the loss that he feels is something no words can express,
As he opens a door where a loved one slept and finds there is no-one to bless.
He makes a new life for his wife and himself, the workaday world must restart,
But first there's a peace to be made in the soul, and a place to be filled in the heart.

A father's a granddad awaiting his turn to cradle a babe in his arms.
To look at the world through their innocent eyes, and surrender himself to their
charms.
To offer advice that is mostly ignored, then passing it off as a jest,
As he, to his credit, remembers in time, that the parents will always know best.
He knows he'll be used when the moment is right, for emergencies no-one has
planned,
For mothers and fathers can't cope with it all, and babies are great on demand.

A father is someone who's cherished in age if the love that he gave is returned,
Reaping rewards for a lifetime of toil and respect that his courage has earned.
There's more time for hobbies, or so he believes, his garden will bloom like a rose.
Perhaps he plays bowls or dabbles at golf, as the tempo of living now slows.
His passion for reading can now be indulged, there are books that he's saved just
for this,
And he drinks in each line, as the words flow like wine, for these are all favourites
of his.

Sometimes he goes dancing with his lovely wife, a marvellous Derby and Joan,
Waltzing away to the end of the day, to that place where his dreams have flown.
A father's a memory after he's gone yet his smiles haven't faded or died,
For he moves like champagne through the blood in your veins and makes you feel
happy inside.

You see his reflection in your children's eyes, a mirror to goodness and truth,
Then see him again, when the years fall like rain, as you did in the heart of your youth.
When Christmas arrives you still feel he is there as you think of the presents he bought,
Those gifts beyond price that he gave all his life, for the word and the deed and the
thought.
It's now that you feel the extent of your loss, the wellspring of love that still pours,
As you look down the years, through the mist of your tears at this wonderful father
of yours.

~~~~~~~~~~~~~~~~~~~~~~

THE CHRISTMAS ROSE

I tried to grow a brand new rose,
The colour black is what I chose.
I built a greenhouse warmed by oil
And filled its bed with rich black soil.

I then cross grafted eighty strains,
I worked it out, I used my brains.
Discarding those I found unfit
And made some progress bit by bit.

In twenty years I grew a bud,
A dark grey shade like farmyard mud.
It had no heart, it held no smell
And at its best it looked unwell.

I spent ten thousand pounds at least
On pesticides and brewers yeast.
Backed all this up with horses dung
And patent tonics by the ton.

A lifetime passed, my hair turned white,
The rose stayed grey, a nasty sight.
My wife and children all left home
And I was left to cope alone.

Well by this time with money gone,
I sold my mansion for a song.
Moved in the greenhouse with my rose
Connected mouth to water hose.

I took off shoes, discarded socks,
Uprooted my best hollyhocks.
Put down my roots in finest peat
And piled fresh dung around my feet.

Through all of this the rose stayed grey,
While I grew blacker by the day.
Soon fibres wound their way round me
And I became a Christmas tree.

A hundred years elapsed before
They opened up the greenhouse door;
And though great force was then applied,
It still took days to get inside.

Men hacked their way through twig and leaf,
For I had grown beyond belief.
Thrust branches through the greenhouse glass
And dropped pine needles on the grass.

But all of this had been worthwhile,
For in my shade now growing wild,
Was found a bush between my toes
On which there grew a jet black rose.

Men stared aghast before its grace
With speechless wonder on each face;
Struck dumb by glory undefiled,
Perfection growing in the wild.

They named this hybrid after me,
"The Christmas Gift" (from Christmas tree)
The world rejoiced and I became
That wondrous thing, a rose's name.

Now they've transplanted me to where
The rose's glory I can share;
And side by side in Royal Kew
We both relive the joy we knew.

With all of this I'm now content,
Though as I'm rooted in cement,
No bush will grow between my toes,
No hollyhocks or hybrid rose.

So if you'd like to honour me,
Place "Christmas Gifts" on my tall tree,
Those jet black roses with the scent
Of horses dung and weak cement.

Thus will my life be glorified,
A people's awe, a nations pride.
Mourn not the flesh I haven't got,
For clothed in bark I miss it not!

~~~~~~~~~~~~~~~~~~~~~~~~

WATCYN WILLIAMS

Watcyn Williams, (Merthyr Tydfil)
Was a lovely preaching man.
Saved lost sinners from the devil,
Lived for love as good men can.
True as steel upon life's anvil,
Watcyn Williams, Merthyr Tydfil.

As he graced his pulpit eyrie,
Penyard Chapel filled with light.
Faith was born within the weary,
Darkest doubts were put to flight.
Fresh from conquest over evil,
Watcyn Williams, Merthyr Tydfil.

As he prayed we felt God's presence,
Walk within those sacred walls.
Touched the Holy Spirit's essence,
Knew the grace that prayer recalls.
Now in age I hear his words still,
Watcyn Williams, Merthyr Tydfil.

Lamp of love in streets of shadows,
Tender words through rough, hard days.
Steps of Christ that this man follows,
Lead us up the hills of praise.
Generous heart that all our wants fill,
Watcyn Williams, Merthyr Tydfil.

Watcyn Williams, (Merthyr Tydfil)
Sick of body, sound of soul.
Sought to keep our lives from peril,
Fought to keep our spirit whole.
Took us with him to his idyll,
Gave his life as Godly men will,
Shared a cross upon a green hill,
Watcyn Williams, Merthyr Tydfil.

~~~~~~~~~~~~~~~~~~~~~

A LITTLE CHILD

A little child might lead us, a little child might guide
The straying steps of we the old and stay close by our side.
We cannot hear for ignorance, we cannot see for pride,
But O! that childhood innocence, could in our hearts abide.

A little babe might teach us, a tender infant lead
Us to a knowledge of ourselves, in every thought and deed.
So we might come at last to truth, and in good conscience plead,
That we are all prepared to go, where little children lead.

~~~~~~~~~~~~~~~~

TO ABERGAVENNY

O! where is that train beloved by many,
That wandered from Merthyr to Abergavenny?
Spanning the valleys on viaducts high,
Sparks from the engine like stars in the sky.
Skittishly dancing on uneven rails,
Climbing stiff gradients, or plunging down vales.
O! where is that train to Abergavenny,
Once they were frequent but now there aren't any.

O! why were they axed, it all seems so silly,
Buses can't go where the roads are so hilly.
Where are the stations where once trains would stop
Low Pant-y-Scallog and high Dowlais Top.
Across Rhymney Common, Tredegar ahead
Haunted by ghosts of travellers long dead.
Queuing for tickets, but not finding any
To take them through time to Abergavenny.

I still remember each Sunday School outing,
The laughter, the singing, the banter, the shouting.
Boarding a train in Merthyr town station,
Full of the joy that I found in creation.
Off to Pontsarn through Heolgerrig and Cefn,
The journey was short, but to me it was heaven.
Yet trains such as these seemed to be two a penny,
As onward they thundered to Abergavenny.

My rides on that train, are journeys I'll treasure.
No words can describe their wonder and pleasure.
Releasing the straps on carriage door windows
Then leaning outside where the steam and the wind blows.
Spouting great verse in the teeth of a gale
Soaked by fat raindrops and hammered by hail.
O! why don't they heed the plea of the many
And bring back those trains to Abergavenny.

Question authority, don't be fainthearted,
In parts of these Isles steam trains have restarted.
Pleasure bent passengers flock to their source
Reliving old dreams as they pack every coach.
Onwards and outwards enthusiasts travel
On railbearing sleepers embedded in gravel
To places once closed to the good and the many
Like stations from Merthyr to Abergavenny.

Where are the people to share in my sorrow
For all that is lost as we enter tomorrow.
Brothers and sisters and friends that I knew
Embarking on trains as guards whistles blew.
With packed picnic lunches and flasks of hot tea,
My mother and father their arms around me.
As joyful we joined in the love of the many
For trains on that railway to Abergavenny!

~~~~~~~~~~~~~~~~~

SAFER UNDERGROUND

My Granny lived in Old Penyard
When cash was scarce and living hard,
But when they pulled the houses down
My Gran was long since underground.

I'll never know what she'd have made
Of living in this modern age
But I suspect that she'd be bound
To feel much safer underground.

I see her sitting in her chair,
Apple cheeked and snowy haired
Along with thoughts of sons who found
A living working underground.

The ragged wick her oil lamp held
Cast flickering shadows on the shelf
Where stood the clock, alas! unwound
The day they placed her underground.

Her world was toil within four walls
Eight babies nursed in woollen shawls
And dreams of happiness were drowned
When two were buried in the ground.

The furthest places she had been
Were Aberdare and Pontypridd.
She never went to London Town
Or travelled on the Underground.

My Granddad died in middle life
But left no comfort for his wife
For there beneath his burial mound
Her love was buried in the ground.

All her days were lived the same
And when the welcome darkness came
To brass framed bed she'd go night-gowned
One stone stepped flight above the ground.

Perhaps the world where she has gone
Will shower all its blessing on
The brave undaunted spirit found
When she was raised from underground.

~~~~~~~~~~~~~~~~~

A RACE OF MEN

They came from a distant planet, that spun round a third rate sun,
  Searching, for ever searching, where the endless reaches run.
Dazzled by myriads of dwarf stars and blinded by cosmic storms,
  Swept by the tails of comets, the splendour of fire transforms.
Forcing the very last frontiers, defended by time alone,
  Seeking, for ever seeking, a race of men like their own.
They came through our solar system, burning their rockets exhausts,
  Telepaths sending out wave forms, probing for other mens' thoughts.
Delicate instruments gauging the right type of atmosphere,
  Computers punching out data, correcting the courses to steer.
Uranus, Pluto and Neptune, Jupiter, Saturn and Mars,
  Ignored by the reasoning people, born on the outermost stars.

But there in the viewports, gleaming, lush green and bathed in light,
  The jewelled mass of Mother Earth, swam sweetly into sight.
Down from the heavens descending, the rocket ships settled to rest,
  In Paris, Rome, London and Berlin, in Moscow and Budapest.
Out from the spaceships doorways, on millions of marching feet,
  Hordes of an alien army poured into each city street.
Their weapons, though not atomic, paralysed civilised man,
  And the war of the worlds was over, before it had really began.

Down in the heart of Africa, where the news was told by drum,
  The patient natives waited for the alien hordes to come.
They waited too, in China, in India, Ceylon and Japan,
  And down to the South Pacific where the Anzac islands ran.
No-one knew what was happening in the Northern Hemisphere,
  But the weeks grew into months and the aliens failed to appear.
Then all of the Southern statesmen, gathering at Singapore,
  Decided to send a mission to treat with the alien foe.
They came to London and Paris, to Bucharest, Moscow and Rome,
  Borne on the wings of jet planes, o'er minaret, steeple and dome,
Down to the city airports, deserted, and so deathly still,
  That the delegates hearts were frozen, and numbed by terror's chill.
Europe was one vast desert, with only the beasts of the field,
  For not a human voice was heard, or sign of man revealed.
The spaceships too had vanished, as if they had never been,
  And the city's streets were empty and the city air was clean.
Buses and cars were rusting, and weeds from the countryside
  Grew through cracks in paving stones, where human hopes had died.
The world was plunged into mourning, and the grieving people wept,
  As out to a distant planet, the alien spaceships swept,
Bearing their human burden, destined to work as slaves,
  'Til welcome death released them, from out of their living graves.

They came from a distant planet, that spun 'round a third rate sun,
  Searching, for ever searching, where the endless reaches run.
Forcing the very last frontiers, defended by time alone,
  Seeking, and finally finding, a race of men they could own.

~~~~~~~~~~~~~~~~

YEAR OF THE CHILD

As we tend our tiny gardens and reseed the fruitful earth,
Do we ever think that children too need caring for from birth.
Do we ever draw the parallel between the plants and them,
That blooms of beauty never grow upon a sickly stem.

Do we nurture minds with noble thoughts, or fill young hearts with love,
Plant values deep within the soul, or really care enough.
Are tendencies to violence pruned, are principles instilled,
Are roots of gratitude refreshed by promises fulfilled?

Is money cheaply handed out when time we cannot spare,
Can children really be bought off by gifts the heart can't share.
As doors are locked against them, shutting youthful hopes outside,
Are we harvesting rejection from a field where love has died?

Can we blame our childrens' teachers for the discipline they lack,
Or yet protect the tender child as youthful thugs attack.
As the elderly are terrorised and vandal hordes run wild,
Do we wipe guilt from our consciences and smear it on the child?

As they roam the asphalt jungle of our neat suburban streets
Do we ever think they might revert to unrestrained wild beasts,
That claw and rend the fabric of the future they all face,
Unless we tame their wildness through the mercy of God's grace.

Perhaps the television set has placed them out of reach,
By drowning conversation in the torrents of its speech,
That shuts the parent off from child so that a bridge is lost
And streams of unconcern remain for evermore uncrossed.

No gardener plants a crooked tree or one he doesn't know,
But roots it deep within the soil that it might upright grow.
Yet as we sow life's garden without following God's plan,
We grow warped, stunted saplings from the precious seed of man.

For children need the touch of hands and not the gardener's glove.
Embracing arms, a Mother's kiss, and eyes that shine with love.
A steadying word, a kindly act, with firmness to restrain
The wild excesses of our youth that only lead to pain.

God grant that we might come to know each basic childhood need,
And rid the garden of the heart of every evil weed.
So we might yet remember, in the years that lie ahead,
That blooms of beauty always grow on stems the soul has fed!

~~~~~~~~~~~~~~~~~

THE GIFT THAT IS TRUE

This from the heart of the boy that was
As the mist of the past clears away.
When the giving of gifts was harder because
We were poorer on that Christmas Day.
When I came down the stairs in your comforting arms
And looked through the love in your eyes,
Where the bright Christmas chains with their magical charm
Wove so sweetly those dear family ties.

This from the love that your son bears you
As the sweet joys of youth come again.
This for the giving of all that was true
Through sorrow and sickness and pain.
This for the wonderful greatness you've shown
That makes you the mother you are.
This for the feeling of Christ in the home
As we sang about Bethlehem's star.

This for the stockings that hung on the line
With the spirit of Christmas inside,
Whilst behind blazed a fire that made the rooms shine
With the glow of the first Christmastide.
This for the making of dreams that came true
As I played with the gifts that you bought.
This for the toil and the hardships you knew,
For the word, and the deed and the thought.

This for the vision that broadened my life
As you gave of your treasures so free.
For streams of redemption flowing from Christ
That poured through your spirit to me.
The fragrance of wonder that sweetened my youth,
Its essence distilled in your soul
From magic ingredients God mixed with the truth
In vessels of silver and gold.

This from the heart of the man I am
As the mist of the past clears away.
This for the way that I love you dear Mam
For the richness of each Christmas Day.
This from the pleasure of being your son
As the blessings of life I renew
May the good Lord reward you for all you have done,
For this is the gift that is true.

~~~~~~~~~~~~~~~~~

ABSTRACTS

If prayer is reaching for the stars,
Could mankind ever get passed Mars,
Or with a human brain to steer,
Pass through Earth's own atmosphere?

If hope is built on random thought,
Would expectations come to naught?
If we unthinkingly destroyed
All common ground and made a void.

If joy is like a rose in bloom,
Then should a weed be clothed in doom?
And could the orchid ecstasy
Be other than a fantasy?

If love's a furnace in the soul,
Would passion glow and burn like coal?
Or would it die when flames depart,
Then turn to ashes in the heart?

If hate brings out the worst in us,
Whom can we like, who can we trust?
For man is made of such base clay,
He throws the best in life away.

If all these abstracts are but true,
Do they apply to me and you?
And if they do, let's make a vow,
To turn away from evil now!

~~~~~~~~~~~~~~~~~

I'M A HUMAN NO MORE

Have you noticed that dogs are great linguists
Who always obey our commands?
Whatever the country we come from
Be sure that the dog understands.
For canines can bark in Swahili,
Egyptian or classical Greek,
Whilst most of we insular British
Have only one language to speak.

A Pekinese yelps in Manchurian
But also in pidgin Chinese,
A bulldog will growl the Queen's English
And Welsh, Scots and Irish with ease.
Poodles are French yapping mostly
And yet with consummate aplomb,
Will translate each sound to Italian,
No matter what country they're from.

I have heard Shepherd dogs howl the chorus
Of Handel's Messiah in Dutch,
And listened amazed to an Afghan hound
Whining in Braille in its hutch.
Retrievers, whatever their nation,
Will sing in a mixture of tongues,
Though this can be hard on a listener,
For somethings not right with their lungs.

I wish that we humans were like them,
Then they wouldn't show their disgust.
They don't think a lot of our species
And tend to look down on us.
They want us to bark out instructions
When taking them out for a walk,
Not only in Brummie and Geordie,
But also in some foreign talk.

The answer of course is quite simple,
We'll have to learn languages too,
Not just a few, but a dozen or more,
Just like our tripehounds can do.
So we can scream louder in Bantu,
Shout insults in gutteral Welsh.
Perhaps you should follow my leader,
I'm starting tomorrow myself.

I think that we humans should ponder
Why dogs are more brilliant than us.
Why we have to use our own language,
While they can bark lots without fuss.
My mother is now eating Bonio,
With Winalot, Lassie and Chum,
But though this works wonders for doggies,
It's not doing much for my mum.

What we ought to do is to watch them,
And copy each sound that they make,
Growl in Korean and bark in Burmese,
At least this should keep you awake.
I am told that dogs have diplomas
Which they are prepared to award
When we can converse in all lingos,
Whenever we travel abroad.

So now I don't sit at table,
But beg on all fours for a bone.
Pant with my tongue hanging out of my mouth,
If a little attention is shown.
I have mastered Castilian Spanish,
Bark rough Russian pronouns galore,
And I have received my diploma,
Thank God I'm a human no more!

~~~~~~~~~~~~~~~~~

WHO

Who sows the seeds for the meadows of time,
Who fits the bark to the larch and the lime,
Who lifts the flower through ashes and grime?
Who else but the Lord our Creator.

Who guides the river from mountain to sea,
Who dusts the pollen of life on the bee,
Who oxygenated this planet for me?
None other than Christ who is glory.

Who fired the sun from a heavenly spark,
Who placed in orbit the moon for the dark,
Who raised the mountain to cradle the ark?
Who else but our God who is giver.

Who guides our steps through the valley of fear,
Who smooths the way when our passing is near,
Who soothes the heartache, and who dries the tear?
If not our dear Lord who is shepherd.

Who speaks through shadows of desolate nights,
Listens to prayer and uplifts to the heights,
Then to His kingdom the sinner invites?
Who else but the King who is subject.

Who knows the fall of a sparrow or dove,
Who cuts the stone from the quarry of love,
Who builds the mansions in heaven above?
None other than God who is father.

Who saves the sinners who come to repent,
Through blood freely shed by the Son He sent,
Who speaks words of comfort through every lament?
Who else but the Lord God who saved us.

Who made the waters of Galilee still,
Who grew the tree for the cross on the hill,
Who loves me now and who always will?
None other than mighty Jehovah?

The earth would be barren, life would be dust,
Wine would be water and bread be a crust,
Kingdoms would crumble and ploughshares would rust,
If we never knew our Redeemer.

Shout hallelujah, joyfully sing,
Christ is our Saviour, Christ is our King!

~~~~~~~~~~~~~~~~

MARMADUKE MOUSE

Marmaduke mouse was a sharp little rodent,
Who entered and left a house in a moment,
Eating the best of the cheese he could find,
But never the mould and never the rind.

Marmaduke sharpened his teeth on fine leather,
Tickled the soles of his feet with a feather,
Combed out his whiskers with twigs from a tree,
And polished his tail with wax from a bee.

When chased by a cat, he'd caper and frolic,
Pretend he was bored and look at a comic,
Then as is the way with the sharpest of mice,
He'd slip through a hole in the floor in a trice.

He watched television and loved Tom and Jerry,
Laughed like a drain and often made merry
On small pools of wine, that spilled from some glass,
That sometimes he drank with his sausage and mash.

He loved lady mice and when he went courting,
He felt so alive, he seemed to be floating.
He won many hearts, for how could he fail
With neatly combed whiskers and wax polished tail.

It has a sad ending, this story I'm telling,
A chip pan was frying and somehow he fell in.
He'd come once too often to steal from this house,
And that was the finish of Marmaduke mouse!

~~~~~~~~~~~~~~~~

WHEN I WAS MOVED BY THE BLOOD THAT LEAPT

When I was a boy with the strength of a bull
(The old man mumbled through lips that were cracked)
The days were long and the nights were full
And every second of both were packed
Measuring strength with labouring men
And the willing girls that I knew of then.

When I was a man with the urge of a ram
(The old man said, with his head in a book)
I bedded the women not giving a damn
If seed should sprout in the flesh that I took,
And here in this valley where I ran free
There's many a brat in the image of me.

When I was a fool with a wife who was not
(The old man said in a voice of despair)
I counted the blessings I hadn't got.
Lived with her temper and tore out my hair,
Made my own bed where I slept all alone
Teased in my dreams by the girls I had known.

Now I'm a widower, free of my chains
(The old man said with a tear in his eye)
I've lost my desires and all that remains
Is the fret of a babe and the urge to cry,
Whilst beddable women and lusty young girls
Shrug me away with a toss of their curls.

When I was moved by the blood that leapt
(The old man whined as he wetted his crusts)
The world was mine but I never kept
The sap in my bones or my animal lusts.
(And they led him away, whimpering aloud
To the place that is rest for the madding crowd).

~~~~~~~~~~~~~~~~~

KING OF THE BEASTS
(An Offal Tail)

When I was a boy, I chewed bread for geese,
Champed oats for horses and other great beasts,
Tested by tasting the slop for the sows,
And nibbled tough grass for the tender gummed cows.

By the time I was eight my teeth were all worn,
My tongue was in tatters, my lips were all torn,
My tonsils were mangled, my gums were so frayed,
That when I did smile all the folk were dismayed.

I asked of my parents if I could be spared
From using my jaws for the meals they prepared,
If food for the animals couldn't be fed
Straight in the mouths that were there in their heads.

This question surprised them, they couldn't believe
That I was ungrateful for all I received,
For if oats and grass could bring beasts to their prime,
Well on the same diet so I could in time.

By the time I was twenty I looked like a sow,
Ran like a horse and moo-ed like a cow.
Clucked like the hens and honked like the geese,
Grunted like pigs and smelled like the beasts.

There is only on fly in this ointment of mine,
My father, the farmer, has this on his mind,
That now it is market time here in North Wales,
He wonders what price I will fetch in the sales!

He measures my withers and lifts up my feet
To see if my horseshoes are tidy and neat.
Ruffles my feathers, looks under my legs
Hoping to find that I've laid him some eggs.

I sleep in the pig-pen and feed from the trough,
Root with the swine, and though you may scoff,
The farmhands all reckon that if I'm shown there,
I'll win all the prizes at Widdecombe fair.

Forgive me for boasting, it's not that I'm vain,
But this is my last chance to tell you again,
I'm ripe for the slaughter, right now at my peak,
And I'm for the block by the end of this week.

They'll serve me at harvest-time, garnished with herbs,
Swimming in gravy and though it's absurd,
I'm proud that I'm chosen for this wondrous feast,
For this surely proves that I'm king of the beasts!

~~~~~~~~~~~~~~~~~

THE TAPESTRY OF AGES

Etched against eternal mountains,
Like a picture in a frame,
Hidden sometimes by death's curtains,
Oft-times shrouded deep in shame,
Lies the tapestry of ages,
Like a book with picture pages.

As we open up its cover,
We see faces from the past,
Father, Mother, Sister, Brother,
There before our eyes at last.
Warm and loving, lost and grieving,
Still in some bright heaven believing.

See them come through mist and shadows,
Marching down the clean bare slopes,
Running through time's sunlit meadows,
Ever searching for their hopes.
As they chase them, some are crying,
Dear sweet Lord, why yet this dying?

Hunter, farmer, peasant, miner,
Gun and ploughshare, pick and spade,
Shining truth as men define her,
Wickedness the devil made.
Warrior days, alive, exciting,
Dreams of peace beyond the fighting.

Now a cleansing wind is blowing,
See it stir the sharp, tough grass,
Now all living things are growing,
Where the ghosts of mem'ry mass.
As death comes and old ones wither,
Babes are born and we forgive her.

Watch the iron foundries crumble,
See the steelworks come and go,
With them pass the proud and humble,
Through time's dark, eternal door.
Close at hand where phantoms rally,
Pits still close down bitter valley.

Slag heaps mount with grim forboding,
Menacing the future years.
Now we see them black and brooding,
Mingling with the grieving tears.
Buried now, where died the fairest,
Time and God have reaped their harvest.

Much too late, the hills are shedding,
Dusty darkness from the coal,
As we watch, the green is spreading,
May it cover loves sweet soul.
Passed where children lost their hours,
Growing now, are funeral flowers.

Now we see the long, slow, healing,
Broken hearts and empty streets,
Lonely souls in chapels kneeling,
Pantglas School with vacant seats.
Where dust's river flowed defiling,
Aberfan is still unsmiling.

Clouds now drift across each picture,
Who can see what life still holds?
Prophecies belong in Scripture,
Man must take what fate unfolds.
We must hope and pray with passion,
While tomorrow's world we fashion.

Etched against eternal mountains,
Like a canvas in a frame,
Hidden sometimes by death's curtains,
Oft-times shrouded deep in shame.
Where the pithead wheel and cage is,
Where time's dark unlighted stage is,
In a book with living pages,
Spreads the tapestry of ages.

~~~~~~~~~~~~~~~~

THESE WORDS OF MINE

To be a new born baby, the only proof you need,
Is nine months from conception, and blossom from a seed.
Of course a doctor's wanted if midwives will not do,
Of every new born baby, these words of mine are true.

To be a happy infant, the things that matter most
Are cuddles from the parents and hearts as warm as toast.
Of course a firm hand's needed, if these won't see you through,
Of every happy infant, these words of mine ring true.

To be an adolescent, you'll need above all else,
A realm of understanding, and a load of commonsense.
With help to solve your problems and fight temptation too,
Of every adolescent, these words are mostly true.

To be a faithful partner, a husband or a wife,
You have to give as well as take, as you go on through life.
There is no other formula, no trick or magic brew,
To be a faithful partner, what I write here is true.

To be a senior citizen, the only proof you need,
Is sixty years, or sixty-five, since first you were a seed.
A pension book, a bus pass, and strength to see life through,
As I'm a senior citizen, I'll vouch that this is true.

To be a people's poet, the qualities desired,
Are skills to bend the stiffest phrase, and thoughts that are inspired.
Of course a soul is needed, with feelings ever new,
But most of all the muse must come, with words you know are true.

~~~~~~~~~~~~~~~~

AN ISLAND NO LONGER

"So you think they will make peace in Ireland"
An Ulsterman once said to me.
"When most of its leaders are looking both ways
And none of them seem to agree".
I looked at this doubter in sorrow
To see in his eyes the morass
That all of the Irish are trapped in
By ghosts of their troubled past.

"They will never confer 'round a table"
This Jonah went babbling on.
"They'll set off their bombs in town centres
Until all the buildings are gone.
The lamb won't lie down with the lion,
The Provos will Protestants kill,
And Loyalist gangs in their anger,
Will blood of their enemies spill".

I saw in his eyes it was hopeless
To try and bring logic to bear.
There had never been peace in Ireland
There weren't any pacifists there.
I thought of the people in Derry
In Belfast and wartorn Armagh
Who were sick of the bomb and the bullet
As all fellow sufferers are.

Yet I can see light in the darkness,
As men of goodwill talk of peace.
When the troubles are troubles no longer
When war and its violence cease.
When all of the past is forgotten
When blame is not set at each door
And Ireland's an island no longer
But joined to the mainland once more!

~~~~~~~~~~~~~~~~~

MY UNCLE TOM

My Uncle Tom was my father's brother,
And yet they were different as different can be.
One was a scamp and a tramp but the other
Was patient and gentle and father to me.

When they were youngsters, Tom was the wild one,
Who lived for the day and caroused through the night.
My father was different, for he was the mild one
Who walked from the darkness out into the light.

They went their own ways through a world that was changing
From war into peace, from death into life.
Both saw the future unfold everlasting,
But Tom took the road and my father a wife.

We saw Uncle Tom when the north wind was blowing,
Nothing to wear but the clothes he had on.
Full of himself and caring for no-one,
Here just for shelter, and then he was gone.

My father was steadfast, unchanged by the seasons,
Never embittered by hardships he knew.
Honest of purpose, his heart had its reasons
For paying life's bills on the day they fell due.

But life is a time for loving and living,
And though my dear father is many years dead,
The years that we shared were full of his giving,
While my Uncle Tom's were barren instead.

Yes! my Uncle Tom was my father's brother,
A king of the road, rough, footloose and free.
He was a scamp and a tramp but the other
Was thoughtful and loving and father to me.

~~~~~~~~~~~~~~~~

THE BEAST IN MAN

Could we look after others
As God looks after us,
Then we would all be brothers
And in His mercy trust.
It's always been a mystery
To me why men should hate,
Or why throughout our history
We kill and not create.

It's time that someone taught us
That love brings joy untold.
That once a Saviour bought us
With blood and not with gold,
So we might live in harmony
As part of His great plan,
For surely He, who calmed the sea,
Can tame the beast in Man!

~~~~~~~~~~~~~~~~

HEARTBREAK SHOP

As you pass its dirty jumble,
Do you ever think to stop,
Wondering at contents humble,
In this mean and dark junk shop?

That old mangle in the corner
Must have worn out some old dear.
Why did no-one think to warn her
That her life was shortened here?

Queen Anne legs on scrubbed top table,
How you must have felt the slight,
To stoic bear on legs so stable,
Costermongers whelk delight.

Easy chairs on broken castors,
Greasy chintz on angled wings,
What a host of tired masters,
Must have pressed your ruptured springs.

In that stairway's shadowed recess,
China knick knacks stand on shelves,
Sentimental, treasured, pieces,
Blue pug dogs and dancing elves.

Greedy children must have sold them,
When their parents passed away!
When they could no longer hold them,
In their hands on Judgement Day.

Who could sell that horsehair sofa,
Black hide shining there, like jade,
Having shared it with a lover,
Where life's golden mem'ries fade.

Low commodes, with sticky varnish,
Potted plants on tripod stands.
Brass framed beds, with knobs that tarnish,
Battered clocks with twisted hands.

Could they speak, these old possessions,
To our hearts their words would go,
With their tales of past transgressions,
Locked behind that junk shop door.

~~~~~~~~~~~~~~~~

THE BRAVE AND THE BEST

I've loved many friends, and if memory ends,
My life will be that much the poorer.
Yet childhood lives on, and is never quite gone,
Of that I have never been surer.
For how can dreams fade, if with joy they are made,
While the shoots of our lives were green.
When each boy was a king, from summer to spring,
And a girl was as proud as a queen.

So I'll never forget all the people I've met,
Forever they'll walk at my side.
And the warmth of each smile, will stay with me awhile,
For who knows how lonely I'll get.
But this I still know, that through life I will go,
Grateful that I was so blest
With such understanding, from lovely companions,
The cream of the brave and the best.

✳ ✳ ✳

THE WORKING DARK

Fifteen I was, and I'd just left school,
A scholarship boy, but a bit of a fool.
Wanting to work and throwing away,
The chances I'd willingly take today.

I still see the hill that I walked down,
To Evans the Bakers, top of town,
The steps going up to Thomastown Park,
And mine downhill to the working dark.

Six in the morning and just about dawn,
And this was the last I'd see of the morn,
Stuck in the bakehouse 'til well after four,
- My memories come from a bitter store.

Six shillings a week, and sixpence to spend,
If this was the start , well where was the end,
With the old school tie of green and red,
Exchanged for the grime of the walking dead.

My very first task that I can't forget,
Was cleaning the dough still sticky and wet,
Leaving the mixer all shining and clean,
And me bad tempered, moody, and mean.

I would fry the doughnuts in trays of oil,
Bringing the temperature up to the boil,
Turning them over to brown the back,
Then spooning the jam in the knife made crack.

Weighing the dough for a loaf of bread,
Tin or Sandwich or Cottage instead.
Lifting each batch to the oven door,
With aching arms and hands that were sore.

Coring the apples and peeling their skins,
Then making the tarts in their little tins.
Or forming the shapes that the cream bag makes,
On top of the fresh baked fairy cakes.

Scrubbing the tables with soap and brush,
Everything done in a frantic rush.
Sweeping the flags and sanding the floor,
And hanging my overalls up on the door.

The darkness come and the long day gone,
The goodnights said and my top coat on,
Then climbing the hill with feet of lead,
With never a cake or a loaf of bread.

Nothing was gained from my weekly pay,
The Means Test Inspectors took it away,
And my Grandma Morris who shared our home,
Had her old age pension cut to the bone.

So I worked for nothing, and nothing was all,
And all that is past is beyond recall,
Except that I gave up the gold for the dross,
And carried my own particular cross.

Fifteen I was, and a bit of a fool,
For my steps led away from the County School.
Chances I had, but I then threw away
All that I might have become today.

I still see the hill that I walked down,
To my very first job at the top of town,
One day I'll take the steps to the park,
And walk up hill from the working dark.

~~~~~~~~~~~~~~~~~

SO ARE WE CHRISTIANS?

So eager are we all to heal, we never see life's scars,
But fix our eyes upon the skies, and gaze towards the stars.
This grubby world we never touch, our feelings are so fine,
That we can wash the dirt and dross out of the heart and mind.

We never see the hungry starve, but chant a mealtime grace.
We kneel and pray each bright new day, yet never see God's face.
The homeless freeze in cardboard tombs, and as they're out of sight
We all can close our bedroom doors and then turn out the light.

The ethnic cleansing still goes on, minorities expelled,
Yet just the same, we shed the blame, in this we've all excelled.
A people waits in agony, its hospitals are filled,
As shells rain down on alien town, and innocents are killed.

So are we Christians in the soul as well as in the flesh,
Are beatitudes just platitudes to give the conscience rest?
Does our concern still come gift wrapped in sermons Christ once gave,
Or do we stand at God's right hand and His creation save?

The third world drowns in squalor, the dust and flies are thick,
Unceasing drought burns all crops out, until the land is sick.
Relief supplies are hijacked, the warring factions maim,
And all of us, without much fuss, still play the waiting game.

As landmines keep exploding, and limbs are left to rot,
While we ignore the sick and poor and those that hope forgot,
It's time we Sunday Christians looked this truth in the face,
That singing hymns, whilst this world dims, will never buy God's grace!

~~~~~~~~~~~~~~~~

AFTER MY BIRTHDAY
Daniel's thoughts, Grandad's words

I have had the most perfect of birthdays,
I have played with my family and friends.
I have jumped on a great bouncy castle
And prayed that this joy never ends.
I have read all the cards that were sent me
I have opened the birthday wrapped gifts
And now I'm surrounded by pleasure
In the knowledge that I'm loved to bits.

How I wish every day was as special
But I'm old enough now just to see
That the love of my family forever
Was shown on this birthday to me.
I think this was planned up in Heaven
By the One whom we worship and trust
Though He is two thousand years older
And gave more than Christmas to us.

I really will treasure each moment
I've shared with you all on this day
For you are all wonderful people
No more than a whisper away.
Hold hands on the road to my future
Stay close through the peace and the strife
Where I will reward you with kisses
And you will reward me with life!

~~~~~~~~~~~~~~~~~

A SEASON IN THE HEART

There is a season in the heart that's always Christmas day,
When shining like that star of old, comes hope to light our way.
Where joy revealed, and kindness shown by all our dancing friends
Will come remembered day by day, until life's journey ends.

There is a corner to be filled in every person's life,
Sometimes by a husbands love, and sometimes by a wife.
For as we circle round the hall and hold each other close,
There comes a perfect partnership that blossoms like a rose.

And as we talk and reminisce, old Christmases return,
For we will not forget old chums whilst yet our candle burns.
We think of those who shared our nights and now forever dance,
In some great shining sequence club, beyond the realms of chance.

There is a season in our lives, a wistful Autumn time,
Where tears of gladness fall like leaves, and bells of memory chime.
And as we glide across the floor, the last great waltz to share,
Then all the world is Christmas day and joy is everywhere.

~~~~~~~~~~~~~~~~~

THERE'S A LITTLE WOODEN CROSS

In a corner of our garden,
There's a little wooden cross,
Where a green, plump budgie, dreams all time away;
But whenever our hearts sadden,
As we feel our sense of loss,
He is with us talking, talking, all the day.

Through the years that were his life's span,
Joey filled our home with gold,
And our hearts were never lonely while he lived.
For the very air would lighten,
As we watched his wings unfold,
To share with us the splendours of his gift.

We have kept his empty prison,
With its long slim chromium stand,
And its presence brings a grief that's hard to bear.
But we turn our heads and listen,
Though its hard to understand,
And we seem to hear his bird talk in the air.

We had bought him as a present,
When my daughter was but five,
And she loved each shining feather in the green.
She would look at him quiescent,
As his words became alive,
And it seemed a special magic moved between.

In a corner of her childhood
There's a little golden cross,
Where a budgie known as Joey never dies.
As she walks her haunted wildwood,
And she bears her tender loss,
I seem to see him flying in her eyes.

For the world of sons and daughters,
Is a realm where parents find,
That the tender ones need sympathy, because,
Far below life's troubled waters,
Lie the deeps of heart and mind,
In some corner of their childhood, by a cross.

~~~~~~~~~~~~~~~~

SHINING GOLD

There is a woman's club I know, whose members fall asleep
When dry and dusty poets come, with words profound and deep.
Their verses don't make sense at all, no tale is ever told,
And phrases used are shabby gilt, instead of shining gold.
Deep in the past I made a vow that I would always write,
Not from the brain but from the heart, to set the soul alight,
And let my words a story tell, to which folk could respond,
Not in blank verse, but flowing rhyme, so that the joy lives on.

For I have found, where'er I speak, that people really care
About the finer things in life that we in common share,
The rock that is the family, the friends we love so much,
And little children of our blood, who mean the world to us.

So when I speak, in guild or club, I blow away dark sleep,
With gales of words conceived in love, though not profound or deep,
And pray my verses all make sense, so that a tale is told,
To strip away veneers of gilt, revealing shining gold!

~~~~~~~~~~~~~~~~

HOW GREAT THOU ART

A blend of verse and hymn

To praise the Lord as we all should
With music or the spoken word,
Is from the heart and wondrous good,
No sweeter thanks were ever heard.

To shout your joy when morning breaks,
Or dress your faith in night's attire;
Is like the melody God makes
On golden harp or silver lyre.

Dear Lord, by all your shining deeds
You make me sing with love unguessed,
As for my soul you intercede,
And though your Word my life is blessed.

How great your works and matchless grace,
How deep your thoughts and how divine,
That you can stoop from Heaven's high place
To save this sinful soul of mine.

*   *   *   *   *

O Lord my God, when I in awesome wonder
Consider all the worlds your hands have made,
I see the stars, I hear the rolling thunder,
Your power throughout the universe displayed.

Now sings my soul, my Saviour God to thee,
How great thou art, how great thou art,
That you can turn from all you've made to me
To build with love, your kingdom in my heart.

~~~~~~~~~~~~~~~~~

FROM GREEN TO GREY

I never thought to see the day
When valleys changed from green to grey,
Or mourn the death of each dark town,
As one by one the pits closed down.

It's not that long I know since when
These pits employed a million men,
Who kept the wheels of commerce oiled
As they in utter darkness toiled.

I saw them go by bus or train
To narrow seams and stalls of pain,
Eight hours of hell, with death to cheat,
In bitter cold, or searing heat.

They never asked for much from life,
A loving home, a caring wife,
Hot water in a cleansing tub,
A pint of ale in some warm pub.

A chance to see the stars or sun
When each hard grinding shift was done,
Or climb to where the world was fair,
To drink the champagne mountain air.

And echoing through time and space,
From them to me in soaring grace,
Their golden voices, sweet but strong,
Caress me still with stirring song.

I never walk these lonely hills
Unless the dreaming landscape fills
With ghosts of colliers long since dead,
Alive once more inside my head.

I never thought I'd see the sight
Of valleys change from day to night.
Or mourn the age that I loved most,
As one by one the pits were closed.

~~~~~~~~~~~~~~~~~

A COMPOST HEAP

A garden, is to me a place,
Where rows of weeds and myst'ries grow,
Yet now and then I show my face,
To sow fat seeds and long grass mow.
My neighbour sees me toiling there,
Comes to the fence and gives advice,
And I am touched that he should care,
To see my garden looking nice.

And then I look passed where he leans,
To where his grass stands three feet high.
See weeds as long as runner beans,
And toadstools mass where roses die.
Within his shed the bright tools gleam,
The key unturned in long locked door,
Each implement a gardener's dream,
No son of soil could ask for more.

A garden, is to me a place,
To pull out weeds and some crops grow,
And yet I'm proud to show my face,
To sow fat seeds and long grass mow.
It's not a picture, but it serves,
We've lost the sin of foolish pride,
And neighbours offered help deserves,
A compost heap in which to hide.

~~~~~~~~~~~~~~~~~

NO WORK OF GOD

I am the dullest man you'll find,
I have no thoughts within my mind.
No great ideas, glowing dreams,
I'm just a moron so it seems.

I cannot draw, I cannot paint,
If offered work I tend to faint.
I'm useless, hopeless, just a fool,
Who nothing learned from life's hard school.

I cannot decorate my home,
If asked to help I always moan.
My garden is to me a place
Where weeds grow with amazing grace.

I turn my wireless on at dawn,
The music plays and then is gone.
The loveliest songs from men long dead
Just turn to ashes in my head.

The greatest sculptures draw no praise,
Cathedrals all offend my gaze.
Whilst symmetry of structured verse,
Is doggerel to me, or worse.

No work of God is worth a glance,
The earth revolves, the planets dance.
Yet still to me the stars are just
Great empty spheres of burning dust.

I watch the ballet, that is true,
But not because of what they do,
But just to make them feel upset
By laughing at each pirouette.

The leader of an orchestra
To me is like a barrister.
I cannot tell them both apart,
And see no difference in their art.

Great authors tend to leave me cold,
I've read no books since I've grown old.
And I will sometimes seethe with rage
At classic plays upon the stage.

I am a Philistine, no less,
Life's finer points are left unguessed.
For I am made of such base clay,
That which was left, was thrown away.

I used to love my wife a lot,
But as time passed I soon forgot.
And though she's never left my side,
I've killed her soul and hurt her pride.

And yet I think there's cause for hope,
I watch each television soap.
To follow every twisting tale
From Brookside Close to Emmerdale.

My brain is dead, my eyes are square,
If programmes clash I shout and swear.
My wife just locks herself away,
Puts out the light and kneels to pray.

"Dear Lord" she says on bended knee,
"Bring joy and husband back to me,
The caring man who won my trust,
Before he spoiled all that he touched".

"Instill in him that vital spark,
Please light his spirit in the dark.
Let finer feelings power his brain
That he might be a man again".

Perhaps this prayer from one so sweet
Will float up to the mercy seat,
Where He who is the Lord of Life,
Will surely listen to my wife!

~~~~~~~~~~~~~~~~~

BEYOND THE REALMS OF TIME

Please pass your baton on to me, my lovely gramps and gran.
Now that you're old you're heavenward bound, which is creation's plan.
I am the son your daughter bore, through her your blood returns,
And I will run life's race for you, whilst yet my candle burns.

For through my eyes you'll see the stars shine fifty years from now.
Feel sun and rain upon my skin, and sweat upon my brow.
Another century's in the wings just waiting to be born.
And through my joy you'll dream new dreams in that millennium's dawn.

I hope and trust that I will run as straight and true as you.
For you were young when youth was fun, and hope still fresh and new.
Oh! how I wish I'd known you then, erect and in your prime,
So I might race free at your side beyond the realms of time.

You were the first to visit me when I was still a babe.
Surrendered hearts and souls that day, who knows the love you gave.
Around each corner of my life I've found you waiting there.
Dear friends and playmates to the end, the wish in every prayer.

And when I breast my final tape, I hope that I will find,
My gramps and gran with arms outstretched upon that finish line.
With both my parents in between as welcoming as they;
And I will pass my baton on to my son on that day!

~~~~~~~~~~~~~~~~~

EVERY DROP OF MAGIC

Dai Prosser hummed, Tom Dando sang,
Mog Edwards gave the drums a bang,
While Blodwen Hughes, all skin and bone,
Blew life into a saxophone.

This was a very strange quartet,
They didn't blend, and yet, and yet,
By some peculiar chemistry,
Sweet music came from them to me.

These were the gentle pre-war days
When speech was soft and song was praise.
When vamped mouthorgans in the street
Made golden summers sad but sweet.

When Sisterhood was company
With hymns and hwyl and cups of tea.
Prayers, guest speakers, Sunday hats
And organists all sharps and flats.

I look behind rememb'ring eyes
Where dreams are born and nothing dies,
To see my yesterdays once more
Through time's eternal open door.

The way my father laughed and joked,
The smell of Woodbines that he smoked.
Those big rough hands that worked for us
And held us all in love and trust.

Within my mind I see him still,
Alive on some beloved hill;
The blazing torch of shining truth
That lit my soul and warmed my youth.

Yes I have watched old values fade,
Seen bright hopes die and blunders made;
But through it all in memory
The good returns from them to me.

Dai Prosser hummed, Tom Dando sang,
Mog Edwards gave the drums a bang;
Whilst I a child in Merthyr town
Drank every drop of magic down!

~~~~~~~~~~~~~~~~

GREAT SCROLLS OF LOVE

I thought that I'd a soldier be
It seemed a worthy aim to me.
The advert said I'd be well paid
Win medals large and wear gold braid.
Full uniform including boots
Much warmer than my civvy suits.
About the hours, well they were vague,
Not crystal clear but quite opaque
As if to mention such a theme
Would my immortal soul demean.
I took it in, this advert droll,
For man is but a simple soul,
And came as fools and morons must,
To join the Army for a crust.

Well for a week it went quite well,
Not much to do and life was swell.
I had my sleep and evenings too
As normal men and women do.
I went for walks with N.C.O's
And quite enjoyed these scenic tours.
Whilst W.O's and R.S.M's
Talked nice to me and I to them.
They made me tea and bought me cakes,
(The kind my wife, and mother makes)
And told me tales about the ranks
That made my heart go out in thanks.
It seemed that this was paradise
Where men rejoiced and no-one cried,
And they who led me from behind,
Were soft of heart and wondrous kind,
Who bent the rules in such a way
That life was easy every day.

Then pinned upon the notice board,
Great scrolls of love we all adored.
Like orders for a ten mile run,
Then nice long marches in the sun.
With knapsacks filled with useful things
Like Primus Stoves with boiling rings,
So after trampling twenty mile,
You then could halt and rest awhile,
To brew up tea and eat hard tack,
Those gourmet trifles civvies lack.

With then a very special treat,
Some ointment for your blistered feet.
The Army know how stiff you get
Through sitting down and getting set,
So kindly post you up for guard,
So that your muscles won't go hard.
Provide a gun for you to hold
To share with you the bitter cold,
And boots to stamp on up and down
To stop your bare feet touching ground.
So thoughtful are these men in charge
That when you ask for your discharge
They say you must a fortune spend
To take the steps toward this end,
But this is done because you see,
They love you so, they can't agree
To let you go without a fight
Because you are their hearts delight!

Well after six hard months of this,
I'd had enough, and I did kiss
The Army and its rules farewell,
(Though buying freedom hurt like hell)
So if an advert meets your eye
For Army life, just pass it by.
Don't be misled, but save your soul
And sign instead upon the Dole!!

~~~~~~~~~~~~~~~~~

IN MARKET SQUARE

I'd never seen this church before,
Or passed beyond its hallowed door;
And yet I knew my God was there,
The day I spoke in Market Square.

I'd come two hundred miles to preach,
Not unto all but into each,
To prove my Saviour God was there
Within the walls of Market Square.

The ladies sat in serried rows,
Arrayed in their best Sunday clothes,
But Christ who all our sins must bear
Saw hearts, not clothes, in Market Square.

They hadn't come for liturgy,
Or just to share a dream with me.
They came because they'd time to spare
To praise their Lord in Market Square.

They didn't seek material gain,
Hope for reward or balm for pain.
They owned no wealth or jewels rare,
Yet they were rich in Market Square.

We sang our favourite childhood hymns,
That neither age or memory dims;
And He who crown of thorns must wear,
Smiled from His cross on Market Square.

We joined in prayer to praise the One,
Who gave us His beloved Son.
That we might one day come to share
The Heaven we glimpsed from Market Square.

I spoke in simple prose and rhyme,
Took listeners back through space and time
To that far hill called Calvary where
Christ saved the world and Market Square.

If ever I go back to speak,
I know I'll find what Christians seek,
For my Redeemer waits me there
In that dear Church called Market Square.

~~~~~~~~~~~~~~~~~

THE HOPEFUL SIDE OF GIVING

On the dying side of famine as the whole world holds its breath,
As lines of bodies, side by side, lie in the arms of death,
There's a touch of desolation, an erosion of the brain,
A vast horrendous sense of loss, a catalyst of pain.
Before the shock waves of their plight have reached our western shores
We watch bewildered on our screens, the seas of festering sores,
The living skulls, the dried stick limbs, the puss lined pools of eyes.
Distended bellies putrefied, child faces dressed in flies,
Babies sucking emptiness from sun shrunk ravaged flesh,
Not feeling in their helplessness their mothers last caress.
The shallow graves like jagged scars run through the arid plains
With only fluttering scraps of cloth to mark their last remains.
As day by day the horror mounts within the caring mind,
The dying side of famine stains the conscience of mankind.

On the hopeful side of giving as the world flies in its grain,
The dedicated famine teams feed hungry mouths again.
From countless homes the money flows, from charities there pours
The means to buy the gifts of life for now and evermore.
Already infants have been saved, the future looks less grim,
As nations rally to the cause and needed food pours in.
But charity is not enough, this caring mood may pass,
As other tragedies unfold to hold our interest fast.
Cosmetic treatment's not enough, starved bellies must be filled,
The land must know the plough again and wells for water drilled.
Resources must be organised, the hungry poor can't wait,
Unless we take swift action now, our help will come too late.
The flame of life is burning low, we look for its rebirth,
The hopeful side of giving brings a new dawn to the Earth!

~~~~~~~~~~~~~~~~~

I WANT TO COME HOME

I want to believe in people, in people I want to believe,
I want to measure their honour, to find if they mean to deceive.
I need to be sure they're faithful, as vulnerable postulants must,
I want to believe in people, I want to repose in their trust.

I want to confide in someone, in someone I want to confide,
Not to a fool in love with himself, or someone with something to hide.
I need the soul of discretion, a man who has no hidden depths,
I want to confide in someone, and know that my secrets are kept.

I long to make friends with someone, with someone I long to make friends,
Not in a weak dilatory way, or simply for my selfish ends.
Someone the future to share with, who want to set my spirit free,
I long to make friends with someone, and someone to make friends with me.

I want to come home to Jesus, to Jesus I want to come home.
He is the measure of honour, commandments on tablets of stone.
He is the friend to confide in, a trust that was paid for in pain,
I want to come home to Jesus, I want to be happy again!

~~~~~~~~~~~~~~~~~

IN OLD PENYARD

In Old Penyard, dark Old Penyard,
Where life was cheap and dying, hard,
Within whose whitewashed cottage tombs
The oil-lamps glowed in airless rooms.

The Red Hill climbed to meet its needs
At one with gardens choked by weeds.
While up above where teachers rule
Your backs rose up to Queens Road School.

Your walls re-echoed coughs that came
From miners' chests that burned like flame.
Your darkest corners damp as death
Joined hands with dust to squeeze the breath.

You kept within your cold embrace
Each stunted mind, each hollowed face.
Denying heat from sun and fire
To light the flame of man's desire.

My father grew to manhood there
With collier boots and clothes to wear,
With sandwich box and cold tea jack
And black pit dust on muscled back.

Where now the homes in rubble lie,
It seems the very stones must cry,
As minute atoms dusty rise,
The only trace of mans demise.

In Old Penyard, dark Old Penyard,
Where dreams were snuffed and lungs were scarred,
Within whose whitewashed cottage tombs
Where all things die and nothing blooms,
The oil-lamps flared in airless rooms.

~~~~~~~~~~~~~~~~~

MY AUNTY DAISY

My Aunty Daisy, who lives up in Paisley,
Is proud of the fact that she's Scottish.
From Burns night to haggis, her country is magic,
Although she's not Snobbish or snottish.
She thrives on hard labour and once threw a caber
So far at the games in the Highlands,
That those who retrieved it could scarcely believe it,
And since have been shocked into silence.

Her spouse is from Holland, but she's a Macdonald,
And like all its members is clannish.
She never seems foreign in tartan and sporran,
But always looks handsome and mannish.
She twirls and she prances in reels and sword dances,
She never indulges in banter.
For she's a great artist who always looks smartish,
Whilst wearing her clan tam-o-shanter.

And my Aunty Daisy will never leave Paisley,
She sticks like a leech to her porridge.
Her country she'll nourish, its flag she will flourish,
For she is more Scottish than snobbish.
And now devolution has been her salvation,
She wants to be M.P. for Paisley.
And when she's selected and duly elected
We all will be proud of Aunt Daisy!

~~~~~~~~~~~~~~~~~

DEAR GOD! YOU MADE THEM ALL

Parody on "All things bright and beautiful"

All things rich and plentiful,
All life forms great and small.
All things weak and powerful,
The Lord God made them all.

He fashioned trees and flowers,
He blew the winds that pass
And then through patient hours
He sowed the earth with grass.

All things herbivorous,
All species, short and tall.
All things truly glorious
The Lord God made them all.

He set the stars rotating
With hands once pierced by nails.
Then went on with creating
The fragile garden snails.

All things clear and visible,
All raindrops as they fall.
All things sweet and kissable,
The Lord God made them all.

He made the mighty mammoth,
He made the bumble bee,
The He rested on the Sabbath,
When He'd created me.

All things bright and fanciful
All serpents as they crawl.
All things drab and colourful
Dear God! you made them all!

~~~~~~~~~~~~~~~~~

DOUBLE GLAZED

One day in the calm of the evening
Just before I sat down for my tea,
The telephone rang without warning,
And frightened the life out of me.
"Hello" said a voice in my earhole,
"Can I speak to the man of the house?
I am offering cheap double glazing,
Either to you or your spouse.
You don't have to pay me a penny,
For my expertise there's no charge.
Small windows are fitted for peanuts,
And discount is yours for the large."
His voice seemed to go on forever,
He hypnotised me I will swear,
I couldn't put down the receiver,
It seemed to be stuck to my hair.
The water boiled dry in my kettle,
The washing machine gave a groan,
My toast was all burned to a cinder,
And still I was glued to the phone.

By now I was feeling quite angry,
The sweat running down from my brow,
A CD had jammed in the hi-fi,
And now it was making a row.
The water I'd run in my bathtub
Began to flow over the top,
And still that double glaze salesman
Went babbling on without stop.
My smoke alarm started to function
To add to my burden of cares;
The water poured out of the bathroom,
And came like a flood down the stairs.

The washing machine blew a gasket,
The microwave started to ping.
A wasp wandered up my left nostril
And frantically started to sting.
The ceiling, much weakened by water
Began to fall down 'round my ears,
The smoke came in waves from the kitchen
And I couldn't see through my tears.
Someone was ringing my doorbell,
Another was at my back door
While water in flow from my bathtub
Had risen twelve inches or more.

And still that great fool of a salesman,
Convinced he was making a sale,
Was holding me fast with his nonsense,
As the light was beginning to fail.

Alarmed by the smoke and the clamour,
My neighbour had called the police.
They in their turn told the army,
Who thought I was breaching the peace.
Soon my small house was surrounded,
And marksmen positioned with care,
Were firing at will through my windows,
Which soon looked the worse for wear.
How it all ended is legend,
You all saw the news on T.V,
As I was swept out through a window
(For water was up past my knee).
My home was a wreck and a ruin,
My life was all tattered and spent
For I had to live in my garden,
And life can be hell in a tent.

And that fool of a double glaze salesman
Had the nerve to come 'round the next day,
For he saw that I needed new windows
And knew my insurance would pay.
So I struck the man down with a hatchet,
Dug him a grave in the ground
Then buried him under the flowers
And hoped that he'd never be found.
But I have to stop writing nonsense,
I see there's an ambulance outside,
And two white overalled attendants
To take me along for a ride.
And I will be happy to travel
To a place where the mad have a home
Which hasn't got double glazed windows
And hopefully hasn't a phone.

The point of this tale has a moral,
Don't end up demented like me.
Pull the telephone plug from its socket,
Before you sit down for your tea!

~~~~~~~~~~~~~~~~~

THE LONDON OF DREAMS

A river flowed into the London of dreams,
Sparkling and fresh from a thousand small streams.
Brimming with fish from bright salmon to trout,
A river flowed in and a river flowed out.

A people moved into this London of light,
Built huts of straw as such primitives might.
Dumped all their garbage where sweet waters ran,
A people moved in and pollution began.

The centuries merged as a vast city grew,
While waste was discharged in the one way they knew.
Refuse was thrown from the banks by the sack,
The centuries merged and the river turned black.

Bacteria invaded the London of crowds,
Spun the Black Plague into fashions in shrouds.
Bodies soon floated on waters once fresh,
Bacteria invaded polluting the flesh.

A river flows into the London we know,
Lifeless and thick with the foul things that grow.
Past grieving for days of bright salmon and trout,
A river flows in and a poison seeps out.

A river will go through the London of time,
Fed by the streams from a mountain of grime.
If we in our blindness contribute the scum,
A river will go and a reckoning come.

A river moves into a London that dreams,
Unnoticed by fools who are sleeping it seems.
Chemical waste and foul sewage will stain,
A river moves in and is buried again.

Scarred by pollution the new mark of Cain,
A river moves in and is branded again.

~~~~~~~~~~~~~~~~~~~~~~

A PRAYER FOR TODAY

Dear Heavenly Father

Send us the power to banish all evil,
Give us the hope that we'll meet you one day.
Lift us, and save us, from wiles of the devil,
Show us the truth, the life, and the way.
Make us forgiving, gentle and patient,
Able to give and not just to receive.
A need to bring love to the heart of this nation,
A gift of true words that will never deceive.
Turn back the clock to a childhood remembered,
Alter its hands to where innocence stood.
Rebuild all the trust we sinners dismembered,
So we might return to a world that was good.
You are the greatest, the sweetest, the finest,
Before the Beginning you thought of our needs,
You sent us a Saviour who blest us with kindness,
Planned every harvest and planted the seeds.
Grant us the will to reflect all your glory,
Make us all shine in the light of your love,
That we might come home at the end of life's journey
To that greatest of welcomes in Heaven above.

Amen

WE WALKED THE SAME ROAD
Ode to a brave departed spirit

I remember the place where my Aunty Crid lived,
By the side of a river whose waters we fished,
In the dark basement rooms underneath Quarry Row,
Where I saw all my cousins blossom and grow.

There was Willie and Thomas and Miriam the brave,
Young Kitty Evans and Eirwen the babe.
Friends of my childhood who shared in my play,
That made Merthyr Tydfil a sweet yesterday.

A few days ago I saw Miriam leave
From her family home to her ashes in Leeds.
We shed many tears and we told many tales,
For we walked the same road from her childhood in Wales.

I saw cousin Thomas - O! yesterday come,
Was this the young giant who dreamed in the sun?
Was this aging father the boy that I knew,
As broken he slumped in the depths of a pew?

And Willie the elder, whom now we call Bill,
His health so uncertain, but lovable still,
Trying to smile through a curtain of tears,
Remembering Mim and the golden lost years.

Kitty was present, but she was refined
By the grace of a King who redeemed all mankind,
Serving as always the family needs,
The Light of the World in the darkness of Leeds.

And Eirwen, dear Eirwen, for she I suppose,
Who once was the baby must comfort all those
Bereaved of a mother, a daughter, a wife,
Who saw the breath pass from the love of their life.

My heart now goes out to the family that grieves,
For Mim was the tree and they are the leaves.
Linda and Peter and Mim's lovely Roy
Who wept in her sadness and shared in her joy.

And to Aunty Crid in the midst of her pain
I offer my faith that we'll all meet again,
Not on this earth where our flesh is but grass
But in God's great kingdom where joys never pass.

So grieve not for Miriam for no-one is dead
While they're kept alive in the heart and the head.
You'll hear her dear voice imploring you still
To climb from the dark to the light on the hill.

I still see that basement wherein you all dwelt,
Remembering the love that we cousins all felt.
Watching it blossom and steadily grow
From the seeds that we planted in old Quarry Row.

~~~~~~~~~~~~~~~~

A FABLE

If storks really bring all our babies,
If gold paves the streets of each town,
If dogs never suffer from rabies,
If leaves never wither or brown,
Then life at its best is a fable,
A fairytale written it seems
By fools who are really not able
To sift what is truth from our dreams.

~~~~~~~~~~~~~~~~

HALLELUJAH SING TO ORGAN

Grieve not now for Rhys Ap Morgan,
Weep not for the brave heart gone.
Play not of death's burial organ,
Raise not voice in joyless song.

Dull no eyes for such bright spirit,
Sport no wreath upon his hearse.
Heap no praise beyond that limit,
Set by God for deathless verse.

Throw no earth on sunken coffin,
Wear no black or purple crepe.
Don no hat to see him off in,
Let no dark plumes sadly drape.

Rhys loved wild, gorse prickled, mountains,
Pebbled brooks and nightingales.
Waterfalls, cascading fountains,
Summer suns and winter gales.

Long legs striding, white hair flowing,
Rhys would dreamlike move through mist.
Wind burned cheeks with vigour glowing,
"Western Mail" in crumpled fist.

He would spout poetic madness,
Make it sound like joy untold,
Then with shining words of gladness
Dress the hills in cloth of gold.

Play no hymns on pipe chimed organ,
Blow no trumpets for the brave.
Toll no bells for Rhys Ap Morgan,
Place no headstone on his grave.

Set instead a block of granite,
On some wild wave battered cliff,
Where the seagull and the gannet,
From their throats defiance give.

Grieve not now for Rhys Ap Morgan
Look past fresh turned graveyard mould.
Hallelujah sing to organ,
Rhys Ap Morgan grows not old.

Hallelujah sing to organ,
Rhys Ap Morgan grows not old!

~~~~~~~~~~~~~~~~~

THE BLESSED SIDE OF CHRISTMAS

On the waiting side of Christmas, before the star has shone,
When Bethlehem is just a place that God has smiled upon,
There's a feeling of awareness, a cleansing of the mind,
As if events to happen there will yet redeem mankind.
Beyond its shadows, to the east, three Oriental kings,
Perceiving greatness soon to come prepare their gifts to bring.
The shepherds watch their flocks by night around the slumbering town,
As angels leave their Heavenly home, glad tidings to bring down.
The stable door is tightly closed, the farmyard beasts are still,
While in its place the manger waits, its purpose to fulfil.
From Nazareth, a man and wife, because God willed it so,
Set forth toward the greatest day the world will ever know.
Watch with me for that bright star to usher in the dawn,
The waiting side of Christmas ends as Christ our King is born!

At the blessed side of Mary, where now the Christ child lies,
A new beginning offers hope through faith that never dies.
There's a dawning comprehension in the hearts and souls of men
That here a kingdom has been built that never more will end.
Before our eyes a torch is lit, to set the world aflame,
A burning knowledge that our lives will never be the same.
Already scriptures stand revealed, their prophecies fulfilled,
Behold the great Redeemer comes, just as His father willed.
Those baby hands that touch our hearts will one day bear the stain
Of nails that drive through tortured flesh, upon a cross of pain.
No need to doubt the shining truth, we see the one true way
By which man goes from death to life upon the judgement day.
As we before the manger kneel, to celebrate Christ's birth,
The blessed side of Christmas brings, God's gift of love to earth!

DO YOU REMEMBER?

Do you remember when the sun,
Bathed mountainsides when day begun,
And warmed the spring of youth within our hearts,
When we would walk the well worn tracks,
And with long poles and sugar sacks,
Make shaky tents the wind soon blew apart.

In schoolboy shorts and cotton shirt,
We played for hours in the dirt
On some old tip that held the coaly slack.
We watered slopes that we might slide,
On metal trays down mountainside,
Till all our clothes were split right up the back.

How we would then to our homes go,
To hesitate before each door,
Anticipating angry parents' blows,
For with our fathers on the dole
Each tattered shirt, each trouser hole,
Meant less to spend on food, and more on clothes.

Do you recall the drifting snow,
That formed, and blocked the street below,
As we lay in our beds those winter nights.
When we would in the morning wake,
To see in each white drifting flake
An endless vista of the days delight.

Of barricades across the street,
For snowball fights, on frozen feet,
Or maybe building igloos from the snow.
The daunting climb to Incline Top,
Where we would on our small sleds drop,
And joyous shouting, down the steep slope go.

Those days when school was out of reach,
When schoolmarms could no longer teach,
Because the roads were blocked for miles around.
We worried not, for this was joy,
Elation born in girl and boy,
As mind remembered every sight and sound.

Cold winter's slow descent to spring,
With feathered songsters on the wing,
And Easter, lovely Easter, still to come.
The days to be, the glorious ones,
With chocolate eggs and hot cross buns,
That we would eat to every last sweet crumb.

Those days are gone, but we remain,
To live their loveliness again,
As haunting glimpses of the past return.
We close our eyes as dreamers do,
And it is nineteen-thirty-two,
Where valley children happy lessons learn.

Those lovely, blooming, August times,
Where youth its own sweet mountain climbs,
To see the joys revealed from that high crest.
That puffing train to Hereford,
Crammed tight with its hop-picking horde,
And countless tea-chests, close together pressed.

Those massive, horse drawn high hay wains,
That met the brown hop-picking trains,
To carry all our boxes to the farm.
The gathering of straw for beds,
With mischief brewing in our heads,
Our parents seeing that we did no harm.

Do you remember when the hops
Stuck fast to wires springy tops,
And pole-pullers would come with their long scythes
To reach and cut the knotted bine,
Where hops and branches intertwine,
And sulphur fell to sting our youthful eyes.

Those sing-song evenings round the fire,
The Welsh hymns sung by happy choir,
The apples roasting on the glowing bars,
The ghostly flit through orchard fields,
To steal the fruit low branches yield,
The magic that was our beneath the stars.

The winded chase by farmers men,
For we were lighter fingered then,
And took his crops from rich and heavy clay.
We took huge swedes or brussels sprouts,
Before we heard their angry shouts,
Then, heavy loaded, ran the other way.

The busheller with whippy wrist,
Who pushed the hops down with his fist,
Until he made what we had picked look small.
My Gran's despairing, stony, look,
As he with power her cribful took,
To only make five bushels of the lot.

Long gone, long done, but who denies
That there before our youthful eyes,
Life changed to gold through every sweet September.
Where autumn sun and autumn rain,
Come back to haunt our hearts again,
Do you remember, still, do you remember?

And if you do, search that dear place,
Where bright on each remembered face,
Such joy shines through, that only heart can know.
In golden walks through memory,
Stretch forth your hands and join with me,
To seek again the love of long ago.

~~~~~~~~~~~~~~~~~

CAUSE TO STOP THE EARTH

Moving through a crowded lifetime, is there time for thoughts of birth,
Are there moments for reflection, is there cause to stop the earth?
Yet can we start this journey if the traveller's not yet born,
Or let others plan our childhood if creation's day we scorn?

Let us look upon the baby, let us see its moving parts.
Will it need a regular service, like our own domestic cars?
Are the compounds that it's made of, strong as steel or soft as mud,
Are the joints all lubricated by the pumping of the blood?

Will the brain direct its thinking, will the thoughts unleashed be good,
Can the cells be truly programmed, is their purpose understood?
Who will share this infants journey, who will guide its every step.
Are the parents good and ready, or are they out of their depth?

Will the travellers move past childhood, are there plans to slow him down.
Are diseases out there waiting, can he swim, or will he drown?
Will there be a golden someone, first to love him and to wed
Perhaps to bear his children on a happy marriage bed?

Will he ever draw his pension, sixty-five seems far away?
Will he lose his hair quite early, is it slowly turning grey?
Will he ever have grandchildren who will sit upon his knee
And will he breast life's final tape, ahead of you and me?

Moving on an endless ribbon, each new circle's made complete,
As a seed becomes a baby and a baby's life is fleet.
Perhaps the great Jehovah should have stopped the spinning earth.
Before creation started and He gave all life its birth.

I am sure, on distant planets there are folk both fierce and meek.
Believing as we humans do, that they are quite unique.
Perhaps there's someone making us just for his private fun.
Who then will throw the moulds away, when his amusements done!

~~~~~~~~~~~~~~~~

THE LONELY FIGURE WALKED

The valley slumbered through the hot June night,
A lonely figure walked down from the hills.
The shadowed moon with edges gleaming bright,
Reflected off the roofs and windowsills.
As townfolk dreamed their dreams between their sheets,
The lonely figure walked their silent streets.

Around him like a mist, his garments flowed,
And all of life lay in his deep set eyes.
Translucently his perfect features glowed,
And through him, stars were shimmering in the skies.
Two thousand years before in Bethlehem,
He'd walked like this into the hearts of men.

He paused before a faded cottage door,
And there in that dark hour before the dawn,
The golden shadow vanished evermore,
As in a bed within, a child was born.
Divinity had come, this time to stay,
To wash two thousand years of sin away.

The valley slumbered through the hot June night,
The cradle of the world between its hills.
A brilliant star, with promise in its light,
Reflected off the roofs and windowsills.
Within their homes, the slumb'ring people dreamed,
And woke to find humanity redeemed.

~~~~~~~~~~~~~~~~

THE GREAT DESIGN

The stand was lit by springtime's glow,
And all was poetry below.
The forwards shoved, the scrum-half passed,
The fly-half took and brilliance flashed,
As with a swerve he dropped a goal,
While joy exploded in the soul.

The Arms Park full of memories,
The gifted players that one sees.
Gareth Edwards breaking blind,
With genius Barry John behind.
The centre passing to the wing,
The brave tries scored as Welshmen sing.

John Williams up to make the line,
The final pass, the great design.
With Gerald Davies touching down,
Another win, the Triple Crown,
With just the mighty French to play,
The Grand Slam but a game away.

We walk with gods who see such grace,
The heart blood quickens, pulses race.
We share with others racial pride,
To store their warmth with ours inside.
And all who watch, the past forgives,
For Welshmen know that Cymru lives.

~~~~~~~~~~~~~~~~

EVERYTHING'S RIGHT IN GOD'S HEAVEN

A cat is a four legged goddess,
A man is a ham-fisted lout,
A moggie will purr as you stroke her,
Then afterwards boss you about.
Felines are lords and fine ladies,
Who treat all they meet with disdain,
And they'll never go out in the garden
If they feel it is going to rain.

Mutton is sheep in lambs clothing,
A lamb is an embryo sheep.
The saddle of one is delicious
The others you count in your sleep.
You must have the one for the other,
For sheep are the mothers of lamb,
So everything's right in God's heaven
As long as one's parent's a ram.

A cow is a calf with an udder,
A calf is a sirloin of veal,
The first will give milk by the gallon,
The second has more sex appeal.
If a cow was as sweet as her baby,
She'd never grow old in her stall,
So we'd have no milk on our cornflakes,
And she'd have no future at all.

A dog is a four-legged human,
A man is a two-footed hound,
And so, betwixt and between them,
A wondrous closeness is found,
A man simply loves to be followed,
A dog would a follower be,
So everything's right in God's heaven,
The best things in life are free!

~~~~~~~~~~~~~~~~

WITH THE NUMBER ONE-TWO-O

O Merthyr! how I missed you,
When I left with Aunty Gwen,
To look for work in London,
Where young boys became young men.
I had toiled in half-price sweat shops,
For eight measly bob a week,
And I smelled of linen cheese cloths,
With their all pervading reek.

My mother packed my suitcase,
And my father felt its weight,
Deciding he would take it,
To the ticket barrier gate.
I could see he felt the parting,
Even more than my dear Mam,
But for me new life was starting
Like the opening of a dam.

O Hounslow how I loved you,
As I saw you long ago,
From that bright red double decker,
With the number one-two-o.
The gold June sun was bursting,
From the shackles of the dawn,
As I left the night excursion,
In the pale of Southall's morn.

Aunt lived in Hounslow High Street,
Over Rego's Tailor Shop.
A many roomed apartment,
With a flat roof on the top.
I shared with Uncle Hopkin,
Uncle Jim and Uncle Len,
A transient world where kith and kin,
Moved in, then out again.

I worked in Maypole Dairies,
Where I had a counter job,
For which they paid a stipend,
Of a weekly thirty bob.
From this I paid my lodging,
With the hardship this entails,
And sent without begrudging,
Small sums to mam in Wales.

O Merthyr! how I missed you,
When I left you long ago.
O Hounslow! how you changed me,
From the boy I was before.
As I left that night excursion,
In the pale of Southall's morn,
The buds of hope came bursting,
From the blossom of the dawn!

~~~~~~~~~~~~~~~~~

THE START OF CHRISTIAN DAY

The new millennium starts quite soon, two thousand years have flown,
Perhaps the second coming dawns and Christ is travelling home.
Prepare yourself to meet His gaze, purge all your sins away,
This is the ending of the dark, the start of Christian day.

He will not come a helpless babe, or be so lowly born.
This time He'll ride in majesty, as Gabriel blows his horn.
All that He promised He will give, once He reclaims His throne,
And many mansions will we share, when Christ, at last, comes home!

~~~~~~~~~~~~~~~~~~~~~~~

THE CLEAN BARE HILLS

From bleak, Welsh, mining valleys, rise
The sweet, the clean, bare hills.
A patchwork quilt to meet the skies,
That every colour fills.
The wild and yellow prickly gorse,
The cool green curving fern,
The grey flecked sheep, the dappled horse,
The black where grasses burn.

The springy turf beneath one's feet,
The trees with tangled root.
The mountain tops where we would eat
The purple berried fruit.
The ancient pile of quarried stone,
Where Morlais Castle stood,
The endless thickets overgrown
That crept from every wood.

The road that rose from fair Pontsarn,
Above the River Taff.
The seven arches graceful span,
The willows' springy staff.
The shaded walks to Vaynor's heights,
With old friends, dear and true.
The whirring wings, the insect bites,
The joy forever new.

Pontsticills' waters shining bright,
That mirrored happy smiles,
The soft pine scented summer night,
The youthful heart beguiles.
The Brecknock Beacons' graceful sweep,
Commanding and serene,
The quick clear pools that we would leap,
To show that we were keen.

The Rushing Gutter's headlong rush
To meet the Cefn Bridge.
The river's quiet settled hush,
Pool Wallt, below the ridge.
Cyfartha Park with castle grey,
Above the Brecon road,
The Pandy clock along the way,
With hands forever slowed.

The Rocky Road to loneliness,
And barren slaggy heaps.
So near to utter loveliness,
The soul within one weeps.
The stain of man on nature's green,
The grubbing in the dust.
The scars where pick and spade have been,
The coal beneath the crust.

And then again the unspoiled slopes,
Swept clear by cleansing winds,
Where youthful hearts redeem their hopes,
And time no longer spins.
Where panoramic vistas show,
The valleys as they ran,
As down toward the sea they go,
Unchanged since time began.

Penydarren Platform's water grey,
Glamorgan's last thin line,
With Monmouthshire along the way,
Part of this land of mine.
Rumney Common's awesome hush,
The rooftop of my world,
The open heath where I would rush,
The stones my young hand hurled.

And there across the valley floor,
The graves of Aberfan,
Waiting and waiting evermore
To hold the seeds of man.
Many's the time I looked across,
At slagheaps black and still,
To see reflected from their gloss,
The school beneath the hill.

From bleak Welsh mining townships rise
The sweet, the clean, bare hills.
The hopes that live, the fear that dies,
The dreaming valley fills.
Touch any heart, search any soul,
Your brother you will find,
With love to make the spirit whole,
And peace to fill the mind.

~~~~~~~~~~~~~~~~

GOD IS

God is the Father, the Spirit and Son,
  Maker of heaven and earth.
He comes trailing glory through all of our lives
  To open the door of His church.
He kneels at our side when we pray in the night,
  The nearer to feel all our pain,
Absorbing despair as He radiates hope,
  Not once but again and again.
He never forsakes us, or turns a deaf ear,
  He asks just one question of us,
If we are prepared to be born once again
  Of the Spirit and not of the flesh.
He's lifted the burden of our earthly sin,
  The ultimate price has been paid,
Calvary looms through the gathering dark
  And we are no longer afraid.
He smiles from the cross as He gives up His life,
  Bequeathing estates of His love,
That we might be heirs to the mansions He built
  In the kingdom of heaven above.

God is eternal, triumphant and power,
  God is creator and king,
Lord of the flowers, sculptor of stars,
  Summer and winter and spring.
Moulder of nations and fisher of men,
  Guide through the valley of death,
Dispenser of mercy, giver of life,
  Blood to our body, and breath.
We read Revelations and look through the door
  Standing open to God's heavenly home,
And hear a voice speaking through trumpets of gold
  From the Spirit who stands by the throne.
We look to the One who is seated thereon,
  With rainbows of stars in His eyes,
And fall to our knees as we're blinded by truth,
  From the dazzling glory that shines.
In front of his presence, an ocean of glass,
  As clear as the crystal of life,
Reflects like a mirror that's burnished by fire
  The wonderful image of Christ.

Carnelian and Jasper are like unto Him,
    The seven lamps of hope are ablaze,
As rumblings of thunder encircle His throne,
    And lightening transfigures His face.

God is the miracle nature unveils,
    Each intricate jewel of snow.
Raiser of waves on the bosom of sea,
    Creator of life down below.
The tug of the moon on the pendulum tides,
    Each minuscule nugget of sand,
Oxygen blown through the gills of a fish,
    The slope of the shore from the land.
He's bedrock to mountains, foundations to homes,
    Builder of infinite grace,
Drawer of blueprints to shape a new world,
    Mover of planets through space.
He judges devotion, not simply by prayer,
    He measures the depth, not the length,
He understands weakness in action and thought,
    And gives of His measureless strength.

God is acceptance of Biblical writ,
    Commandments by which we should live.
Decency wrapped in a mantle of truth,
    And trust like no other can give.
He never deserts us, or turns us away,
    His patience is worlds without end.
He hears us revile Him and crown Him with thorns,
    And yet is the first to befriend.
We have no conception of all that He is,
    His greatness encompasses time,
And yet on our brow as we beg of His grace,
    The touch of His lips is divine.

God is the conscience that nags at the mind
    When we know what we're doing is wrong,
The blessed remembrance of all that is good,
    That keeps all our purposes strong.
The essence of purity riding the breath
    That stifles foul language at birth,
Instiller of principles deep in the mind,
    The sole arbitrator of worth.

Each Christmas He kindles the Bethlehem star,
  Each Easter He climbs Calvary,
Then rolls back the stone that is walling Him in,
  That we might forever be free.
God is the flashing of gossamer wings,
  The pollen of life on a bee.
Colour in rainbows, the blackness of space,
  And beauty we see in a tree.
His facets are endless, reflecting His love,
  His ways are unfailingly right,
He was and He is, and will be evermore
  'Til the sun and the stars fade from sight.
He steadies our footsteps as stumbling we go,
  He knows it is human to stray,
And reaches with hands that were wounded by nails,
  To set us once more on the Way.

God is companion, protector and friend,
  God is the maker of truth.
His freshness of innocence seen in a child,
  The bittersweet yearnings of youth.
He's joy in the morning, the singing of birds,
  The maidenlike, blushes of dawn,
Thunder and lightening, life-giving rain,
  And peace in the eye of a storm.
He speaks from each page of a glorious Book
  In words that are fashioned from pain,
He wills that we wash in the blood of the Lamb,
  The kingdom of heaven to gain.
He walks in a garden and asks if the cup
  Of death can be dashed from His lips,
But when He is answered within His own soul,
  The blood and the bitterness sips.
It wasn't for nothing He suffered and died,
  The tide of His life lapped a shore,
Where all that would happen because of a cross,
  Would change what had happened before.

God is the answer to all of our needs,
  And God is the sum of our parts.
He takes us, and makes us, the gems in His crown
  And lodges His peace in our hearts.

He's gentleness found in the souls of our sons,
Courage our daughters must find.
The selfless devotion in husband and wife,
A vision of faith in the mind.
He's wistfulness left in the wake of a dream,
A heartbreaking feeling of loss,
As if we remember a babe in a stall,
And a Saviour who hung on a cross.
He's angel and shepherd, wisemen with gifts,
Keepers of inns without rooms.
Mary and Joseph, Herod and priests,
Soldiers who guarded His tomb.
Nothing that is can be kept from His touch,
The net that He casts is enough
To gather the atoms of all living flesh,
In the infinite reach of His love.
We are the shadows He leaves in His wake,
The flickering images seen,
As those who are nothing gain substance and form
From places His presence has been.

God is the rustling of leaves in the wind,
The green at the heart of the grass.
The yellow of daffodils, blue of the sky,
And prisms reflected in glass.
He looks through the window of each human eye
To see if we dwell in His house,
And knows if we're there by the things that we do,
Not the words that escape from the mouth.
He's never unwilling to measure His strength
With the devil incarnate in hell,
To save what is good in the spirit of man
From the angel of darkness who fell.
He stamps on temptation, deflates foolish pride,
Demolishes envy and greed,
Stands with His back to the wall that surrounds
The Kingdom He'll never concede.
He thinks we're worth saving, no matter the cost,
No thought could be greater than this,
That He is the Saviour who'll always be ours,
As we are incredibly His.

God is the image in which we are cast,
   Materials from which we are made,
Eden and wilderness, Abel and Cain,
   Light everlasting, and shade.

He spans the broad spectrum of all human thought,
   He sees every virtue and sin,
Exploring the labyrinths deep in the brain,
   For nothing stays hidden from Him.
Sometimes He's saddened by that which He finds,
   The sacrifice we have betrayed,
But lives in the hope that the damned who are lost
   Will soon by His mercy be saved.
Each prodigal son who returns to His arms,
   Each sheep that comes back to the fold
Is greeted with joy, no mortal can know,
   And love that will never grow cold.

God is the Christ who was bruised in our stead,
   Crushed and then finally slain.
A lifetime of loving, surrendered for us,
   Perfection rewarded with pain,
Oppressed and afflicted, He spoke no defense,
   But carried our sorrows and grief,
Pierced for transgressions He didn't commit,
   Murdered for our unbelief.
Despised and rejected by those He would save,
   Familiar with suffering and loss.
Bearer of scars of the whip and the nails
   And bowed by the weight of a cross.
Marked by iniquities never His own,
   Ridiculed, slandered and crowned,
Not by a diadem fashioned in heaven,
   But plaited with thorns all around.
He towers in majesty over the world
   Yet humbly He washes our feet,
And hurries to greet us with arms opened wide
   The least of his subjects to greet.

God is the hinge on which everything moves,
  The door that is always ajar.
The hub around which the universe turns,
  The planets that circle a star.
The limitless void is as nothing to Him,
  He made it one purpose to serve,
That in one small corner, a part of Himself
  Could walk on a wakening earth.

He signposts the highway by which He'll return,
  He gives us a glimpse of His plan,
That we might prepare for the Kingdom to come,
  Not the passing republics of man.
No cross will arise on Jerusalem's hill,
  No mourners will stand by a grave,
He'll come with His legions of angels and saints,
  The ranks of the faithful to save.
Nothing can hinder that ultimate end,
  His church will triumphantly rise,
And all who repent of their foolish desires
  Will come to the One who is wise.

God is eternity biding its time,
  The grace of the Lord Jesus Christ,
Goodness immaculate, free from all sin,
  The Way, the Truth and the Life.
Before the beginning His consciousness was,
  He'll be there long after the end.
Alpha, Omega, first to the last,
  Our personal Saviour and friend.
And as we walk heavenward, our eyes to the stars,
  As sinners, repentent, all must,
We'll come to a God we've been longing to see,
  And find He is waiting for us!

~~~~~~~~~~~~~~~~

THE LAST CURTAIN

I've come to the end of this poetry book,
With sadness I write the last page.
I feel like the cast at the end of a play,
As they finally exit the stage.
The drama is over, the last lines declaimed,
It's time for the last curtain call.
You've been the best audience that I've entertained,
I hope I've kept faith with you all.

I'm not too ambitious, I don't expect fame,
I just want to share what I feel.
Those moments of magic that studded my life,
And made my existence ideal.
Each one of these poems that I have now sired
Were warmed by my blood as they grew,
Then nurtured and fed in the way I desired
And given, with pleasure, to you.

I've likened this book to the play of my life,
For those near and dear are the cast.
Its pages paint scenes that bring back to me
All the love that we shared in the past.
It has a beginning, a middle, an end,
The story it tells is my own.
Where each of its characters speaks as a friend,
Wherever the drama is shown.

The lights are now dimmed, the sets all removed,
The programme consigned to a drawer.
'Twas good while it lasted, the actions superb,
And maybe some watched it in awe.
There'll be a re-run that others might see,
Though critics may tear it apart,
Yet I can but hope there are others like me,
Who will give it a place in their heart!

BIOGRAPHICAL NOTES

Ray Harman was born on June 27th 1922, the son of a steelworker, in Penyard, Merthyr Tydfil, Glam. He has been writing poetry for the best part of his life and seen much of it published in books, magazines and newspapers.

He has performed on stage with Victor Spinnetti, Glyn Houston, Stan Stennett, Lewis Jones, Mari Griffiths and many more well known Welsh entertainers - all of whom have placed on record their admiration for his work. Welsh minstrel Max Boyce has been a fan of Ray's since hearing his work performed on television and is happy to endorse this present anthology.

Ray has had three collections of his poetry published over the years. The first, under the title 'Songs of the Valley', appeared in the 'Anglo Welsh Review' in the spring of 1974. The second 'Poems and Pictures' was produced in South Africa in 1987, and the third, 'A Resounding Voice', was published by Horseshoe Publications in 1995. Since then he has broadcast on the BBC from London, reading poems from 'A Resounding Voice' and has taken his unique blend of poetry and lyrical prose to entertain audiences throughout the Home Counties.

He lists his hobbies as poetic composition, sequence dancing, entertaining and baby sitting his beloved grandchildren.

Ray acknowledges that much of his success can be attributed to his dear friend and publisher John C. Hibbert, who has shown a remarkable faith in his talents and has produced two of his poetic anthologies. The original edition of 'A Resounding Voice' and its subsequent reprints have sold to the last copy, and it is Ray's hope that the successful partnership of poet and publisher will continue to flourish and endure.

Ray is on the panel of speakers of the National Association of Womens Clubs, the Network of Methodist Fellowships and many other guilds and clubs throughout the Home Counties.